Cemeteries of the City of Newport News

Formerly Warwick County Virginia

Courtesy of Newport News Public Library

Cemeteries of the City of Newport News

Formerly Warwick County Virginia

Compiled and edited by
Barry W. Miles and *Gertrude Stead*

HERITAGE BOOKS
2007

HERITAGE BOOKS
AN IMPRINT OF HERITAGE BOOKS, INC.

Books, CDs, and more—Worldwide

For our listing of thousands of titles see our website
at
www.HeritageBooks.com

Published 2007 by
HERITAGE BOOKS, INC.
Publishing Division
65 East Main Street
Westminster, Maryland 21157-5026

Copyright © 1999 The Hugh S. Watson Jr. Genealogical Society of Virginia

Other books by the author:

Abstracts of the Wills and Administrations of Accomack County, Virginia, 1800-1860
Barry W. Miles and Moody K. Miles, III

Cemeteries of the City of Hampton, Virginia, Formerly Elizabeth City County
Barry W. Miles

Marriage Records of Accomack County, Virginia, 1854-1895
(Recorded in Licenses & Ministers' Returns)
Barry W. Miles and Moody K. Miles, III

Tombstone Inscriptions of Upper Accomack County, Virginia
Mary Frances Carey with Moody K. Miles, III and Barry W. Miles

All rights reserved. No part of this book may be reproduced or transmitted in any form or by any means, electronic or mechanical, including photocopying, recording or by any information storage and retrieval system without written permission from the author, except for the inclusion of brief quotations in a review.

International Standard Book Number: 978-0-7884-4396-8

ACKNOWLEDGMENTS

The compiler, Barry W. Miles, would like to express his appreciation to those who helped make this book possible. First to the Virginia State Library & Archives for access to the Virginia Historical Inventory transcription done under the Works Progress Administration in 1936 and 1937. The value of these records are immeasurable because some of the tombstones have since disappeared due to development, vandals and /or deterioration. The Tidewater Genealogical Society would like to thank all the property owners and overseers of cemeteries on their properties or under their authority, for allowing the transcription of the tombstones in these cemeteries, graveyards or family burying grounds. Thanks to Mr. Hutchinson and Boy Scout Troop # 108, for their work on Denbigh Baptist Church Cemetery, First Baptist Church Denbigh Cemetery, Newport News Primitive Baptist Church Cemetery and Providence Mennonite Church Cemetery.

This book is made possible because of the work done by Gertrude Stead. Thanks for the many hours of research, field trips to locate cemeteries, transcriptions of tombstones, photographing of these cemeteries, and the review and editing of data compiled and input into a word processing program. She is truly an expert on Warwick County, having been raised in Warwick County and having lived most of her life on the Peninsula. I want to thank my wife, Leslyn L. Miles, for an understanding of the many hours I have toiled in compiling information and putting the data in a word processor program, indexing, and producing a final book format.

Barry W. Miles
120 Cherwell Court
Williamsburg, Va. 23188

March 1998

TABLE OF CONTENTS

Acknowledgment v

Table of Contents vii

List of Illustrations xi

Introduction xiii

Abbreviations xvii

First Baptist Church Denbigh 1

Benns' Road Cemetery or Marrow Cemetery, "Oakville" Farm 14

Blooming Baptist Church Cemetery 16

Cary Burying Ground, "Peartree Hall" 18

Cemeteries Destroyed, Moved, Not Found or Access Denied 22

    1st Baptist Church Morrison Cemetery 22

    Camp Butler Federal Prison Camp, Confederate 22

    Confederate Graveyard Site 22

    Gibbs' Family Graveyard 23

    Huntington Heights Burials 24

    Newport News Farms Cemeteries 24

    New Apostolic Church Cemetery 25

    North Brickyard Road Burials 25

    Oyster Point Road Burials 25

    Potters Field 26

    Russell Graveyard 26

>   Sarah B. Watson Grave 27
>
>   Walls' Slave Graveyard. 28
>
>   Wilson Family Graveyard 30

Cole Family Graveyard 31

Curtis Cemetery 34

Garden of Eden, Peninsula Korean Baptist Church, Garrow Graveyard 40

Denbigh Baptist Church Cemetery 42

Gambol Graveyard 65

Garrow Cemetery 67

Harwood Cemetery 68

Lebanon Church of Christ Cemetery 71

Lee Graveyard 89

Maney Cemetery 92

Miles Cary Cemetery 98

Miles Cary Cemetery at "Richneck" 100

Mulberry Island Cemeteries 103

> Carter Crafford Family Cemetery 104
>
> Crafford Family Slave Cemetery 107
>
> Crafford Family Cemetery, Fort Crafford 107
>
> Crafford Family Slave Cemetery, Fort Crafford 107
>
> Curtis Family Cemetery 107
>
> Dozier Road Cemetery 109

- Fitchett Family Burial Ground 111
- Jones House Burial Ground 111
- Mulberry Island Cemetery, ... 111
- Nettles Family Cemetery 111
- Saxon's Gaol - Possible Graves 111
- Work Progress Admin. Cemetery, WPS and FERA Burials 112

Newport News Primitive Baptist Service Church Cemetery [formerly Morrison Episcopal] 115

Peninsula Memorial Park 118

Providence Mennonite Church Cemetery 123

Warwick Memorial Church Cemetery 128

Warwick River Mennonite Church Cemetery 130

Wilber Graveyard 133

Young Family Cemetery 135

Index 137

LIST OF ILLUSTRATIONS

First Baptist Church Denbigh Cemetery 12,13

Slab type stone of Mary A. T. Marrow 15

Blooming Baptist Church - African American 16

Blooming Baptist Church Cemetery 17

Tombstone of J. H. Montague 17

Carey Burying Ground "Peartree Hall" 21

William Cole tombstone with Cole coat of arms 33

Broken slab tombstone of the Cole family 33

Curtis Cemetery 34

Tombstone of Miles G. Curtis 34

Tombstone of Daniel C. Patrick, C.S.A. 35

Tombstone of Martha J. Charles, wife of E. C. Charles, 1813-1890 35

Tombstone of D. P. Jones 41

Tombstone of Takeharu Sakai 41

Denbigh Baptist Church Cemetery 44

The Gambol Graveyard as it looked in 1997 66

Harwood Family Cemetery Endview 68

Harwood Garden Cemetery 68

The Lebanon Christian Church Cemetery 86-88

Allen Davis 91

Robert Lewis Davis, Killed 1865 91

Maney Cemetery 92

Tombstone of Mallory Maney 97

Miles Cary (the first) 99

Richneck Plantation Historical Marker 101

Tombstones of Miles Cary II and Wife, Mary Milner Cary 102

Tombstone of Rev. Thomas Wright, Dozier Road 110

Tombstone of Samuel L. Armfield, Jr. 110

Works Progress Administration Cemetery 112-114

Newport News Primitive Baptist Service Church and Cemetery 116

Tombstone of Robert James Gambol and Martha E. Amory Gambol 117

Tombstones at Newport News Primitive Baptist Church Cemetery 117

Peninsula Memorial Park, Nettles Drive entrance 121

Peninsula Memorial Park, Old Section and New Section 122

Providence Mennonite Church Chapel 126

Providence Mennonite Church and Cemetery; Historical Marker 127

Warwick Memorial Cemetery and Church 129

Warwick River Mennonite Church Cemetery 132

Young Family Cemetery 136

INTRODUCTION

The purpose of this book is to preserve for the record the tombstone inscriptions of known cemeteries in what is now the City of Newport News, previously Warwick County. It is our intent that these tombstone inscriptions will assist genealogists and historians in their future endeavors.

A brief history of Newport News / Warwick County boundary lines and annexation.

1607 - Jamestown settled by the English. (From the records of the Virginia London Company Records)

1617 - Virginia Council Order established four great divisions designated: Incorporation, James City, Charles City, Henrico and Kecoughtan. (Susan Myra Kingsbury - Records of the Virginia Company of London)

1619 - Kecoughtan changed to Elizabeth City - Kecoughtan included the land between the James and York Rivers, north to Skiffe's (Keith's) Creek and the New Poquoson River, to the territory on the south side of the present day Hampton Roads, to the Atlantic Ocean and reached to the Nansemond River. (Henning Statutes at Large, Vol. III, p 95 & London Company Records, Vol. III, p 161)

1631 - Warwick River Area established at monthly court. Monthly court was authorized for Charles City and Elizabeth City, March 1624.

1634 - Establishment of eight shires: Elisabeth City, Charles City, Accawmach, Warrasquyoake, James City, Charles River (York), Henrico and Warwick River. (Hennings Statutes at Large, Act 13, p 249)

1642/43 - Assembly act authorized to be called the County of Warwick. Bounds of the county: "From the Mouth of Keith's (Skiffe's) Creek up along the lower side of the head of it, including all the dividend of Mr. Thomas Harwood, Mulberry Island, Stanley Hundred, Warwick River, With all the land belonging to the Mills and so down to Newport News with the families of Skowen's (Scones's) Damms." (Henning Statutes at Large, Act 25, p 250)

1882 - January 28, Approved by the general assembly: "That part of the dividing line between the counties of Warwick and Elizabeth City that runs from the upper angle in said line near Scones Dam road, towards and through the proposed City of Newport News, to a point on the James River above the mouth of Newport News Creek , shall be changed in the following manner, to-wit: From that point in the line near right angle to the south, it shall run northwardly on a line parallel to the streets of said city, to a point at which said line would intersect with an extension of the central in what is laid down on the map of

Newport News as Elm avenue; and thence along said extended line and the same, to the present line of Elizabeth City County, in Hampton Roads. The line here described shall hereafter be a part of the dividing line between the said counties of Warwick and Elizabeth City."

1896 - June 16, (Approved) - "An Act to Incorporate the City of Newport News in county of Warwick and provide a Charter therefore. Beginning at a point at low-watermark on James River, where center line of Fiftieth Street intersects the same; thence easterly along the said center line of Fiftieth Street to the westerly boundary line of the right of way of the Chesapeake and Ohio Railway Company; thence following the said right of way southwardly to the center of Thirty-sixth Street; thence easterly along the said center of said Thirty-sixth to the intersection of the center line of Madison Avenue; thence along the said center line of Madison Avenue to the center line of Thirty-Second Street; thence along the said center line of Thirty-second Street; eastwardly to the boundary line between the counties of Elizabeth City and Warwick; thence with said county line southward to the intersection of the center line of Twentieth Street; thence along said center line of Twentieth Street westerly to the easterly side of the right of way to the Chesapeake and Ohio Railway Company, being three hundred feet westerly from Warwick Avenue; thence along the said easterly side of the right of way of the Chesapeake and Ohio Railway Company to a point in the line with the southeastern boundary line of George B. West's property produced in a northeasterly direction; thence in a southwesterly direction along the said line of George B. West line to low-water mark on James River; thence along the low-water mark northerly to the point of beginning, in accordance with the map of the City Newport News, made by W. A. Post, civil engineer; all of the said territory being in the County of Warwick, shall be deemed and taken as the City of Newport News, and said boundaries shall be construed to embrace all wharves, docks and other structures of every description that have been or may hereafter be erected along said waterfront."

1900 - Act of Assembly - 50th Street to Center of 57th Street (from Warwick County).

1917 - January 17, Effective - "Extend the southerly boundary from the center line of 20th Street, between the center line of Marshall Avenue and the C & O Railway Company's right of way, to low-water mark on Hampton roads and the James River." (From Warwick County)

1920 - April 15, Effective - North of 57th Street extending to a point one hundred feet north of the northerly building line 64th Street. (Annexed from Warwick County)

1921 - January 1, Effective - "Area on the east from a line about half way between Oak and Parrish Avenues to the meandering Of Salter's Creek and the West Branch of that creek, and extending from the center line of 20th Street to the center line of 32nd Street projected."

1921 - June 1, Effective - "Area bounded by the right of way of the Hampton Branch Line of the C & O Railway Company on the north and the formed City limits line on the south, which followed the center line 36th Street and easterly to Marshall Avenue, thence southerly along the center line of Marshall Avenue to 32nd Street and thence easterly along the center line of 32nd Street to easterly City limits line, where it intersected the westerly boundary line of Elizabeth City county." (annexed from Warwick County)

1927 - January 1, Effective - Formerly the town of Kecoughtan, Elizabeth City County. extended the City's eastern boundary line to the center of Pear Avenue.

1927 - February 27, Effective - Corrected oversight at the time of the annexations of the town of Kecoughtan. Brought in a small jib of land lying between the easterly side of Salter's Creek and the westerly boundary of the town of Kecoughtan. (Annexed from Elizabeth City County)

1940 - December 5, Effective - Section of Warwick County lying south of the center line of 29th Street, east of the center line of Marshall Avenue and Marshall Avenue projected and bounded on the south by Hampton Roads and on the east by the westerly boundaries of the territories included in annexations numbers.

1952 - July 16, Referendum by the people, Warwick County became incorporated as the "City of Warwick" in accordance with a charter granted by the Virginia Assembly. (Warwick: the city and its Government)

1956 - July 1, Newport News and City of Warwick consolidated to become the "City of Newport News". (Newport News, 1607 - 1960)

Footnote:
 1. There seems to be a difference of opinion on the boundary line for James City Incorporation in the year 1617. In the book "Conquest of Virginia: The Third Attempt" by Conway W. Sams, pages 311-312, the author stated -" From Chickahominy down the river to Newport News and the line dividing Isle of Wight and Nansemond Counties, we take to be the area given to James City County".

Sources of Information:

Susan Myre Kingsbury - Records of the Virginia Company of London. Documents, 1, 1607 - 1622.

W. W. Henning, Statues at Large.

Index to Enrolled Bill, General Assembly, 1776 - 1910.

Acts of Assembly (1881 - 82) Regular and Extra Session, p 43.

Annie L. Jester - Newport News, 1907 - 1960.

Alexander C. Brown (ed. by) - Newport News, 325 Years.

Warwick: The city and it's Government

Conway W. Sams - The Conquest of Virginia; the Third Attempt, 1610 - 1624.

A note of caution, there are words that will appear to be misspelled. When information is transcribed from tombstones, the spelling is given as it is on the tombstone, to the best ability of the transcriber. All genealogists and historians using the information in this book should follow the golden rule for genealogists: Do not accept the enclosed information as the final authority. Go to the original source and read the information for your research.

Barry W. Miles and Gertrude Stead

ABBREVIATIONS

Ave.	Avenue
b.	birth
Bapt	Baptist
Capt	Captain
Ch	Church
Chp	Chapel
Ck	Creek
Co	County
d/o	daughter of
dec'd	deceased
Dr	Doctor
d/s	double stone
FN	Free Negro
f/s	foot stone
h/o	Husband of
Isld	Island
Jr	Junior
ME	Methodist Episcopal
Meth	Methodist
Mkr	marker
r/o	residence of
Rd	Road(s)
Rev	Reverend
s/o	son of
Sr	Senior
w/	with
w/o	wife of

INFORMATION

It will be noted that 'unreadable' and 'unknown' are used in transcriptions herein. Unreadable is when the transcriber is unable to read the inscription on the stone. Unknown is when there is a vault without a marker.

CEMETERY LOCATIONS

After the street address, there is a number in parentheses. This number is assigned to the cemetery to help locate it on the Newport News City map, which is folded in the back of this book. Also, there is a number in brackets. This number refers to map co-ordinances, useful in locating the cemetery of interest. These numbers have been placed as close to the location as practical. The exact location is not always known on the lost, moved or destroyed cemeteries.

FIRST BAPTIST CHURCH DENBIGH
CAMPBELL ROAD (3) {K 20}

MARROW
Carter B.
Dec. 24, 1873
Aug. 28, 1944

MARROW
Roxanna A.
May 7, 1882
Jan 17, 1970

Mrs Christean W. WHITE
Died May 13, 1939

Deacon J. M. WHITE
Born June 2, 1868
Died June 23, 1957

George Dewey
HOPSON
Oct. 20, 1900
Aug. 4, 1925

J. M. HOPSON
Mar. 20, 1882
Sept. 21, 1918

Mother
Mary
BROWN
May 10, 1845
Jan. 12, 1926
Sleep & Take
thy rest

Lelia M. ROBINSON
Mar. 17 1886
Feb. 25 1976

William P.
HUGHES
Born Mar. 24, 1886
Died May 11, 1927
Though Thou Art
Gone
Fond Memr'y Clings
to thee

Mrs. S. HUGGUNS
Born 1866
Died Dec. 18, 1932
Gone But Not
Forgotten

Saac C. HUDGINS
Born April 13 1927
Died Jan. 7 1944

Thomas HUDGINS Jr
Aug. 7, 1887
Oct. 2, 1956

Enniel L. HUDGINS
June 26, 1892
July 8, 1965

Thomas HUDGINS III
Oct. 3 1930
March 9 1986

Lueatta C. JENKINS
May 12, 1894
Dec. 14, 1969

Janna WHITE
March 2 1802
March 21 1884

Joseph E.
BEVERIDGE
Oct. 16, 1896
Nov. 29, 1976

Bernice W. BROWN
Feb. 2, 1922
May 5, 1973

Jimmie P. WELLS
Jan. 12, 1914
April 24, 1945
In Loving Memory

Laura G. WELLS
May 10 1877
Oct. 20 1959
In Loving Memory

Henderson WELLS
Dec. 26, 1863
April 4, 1961
In Loving Memory

Leola V. WATKINS
1898   1989

Martha REED
Born 1875
Oct 6 1948

James
Andrew DODWON
Born Sept 16 1875
Died Sept 10 1937

Catharine SMITH
Oct 24 1917

Unreadable

Lucy A. TALTON
April 28, 1892
July 26, 1980

Bernice A. WILSON
Nov 16, 1930
Jan. 16, 1982

Unknown

Lottie V. ROBINSON
Sept. 9, 1915
Oct. 7, 1977

Dorothy REED
SCOTT
Aug. 19, 1932
June 27, 1960

Thomas BANKS
29 Jan 1886
28 Oct 1918

Samuel
MALLACHI
Mar 1 1893
Apr 20 1923
At Rest

Mammie C. HARRIS
Nov. 4, 1892
July 8, 1971

William HARRIS
Jan. 25, 1891
Jan. 4, 1984

George HUDSON
Born Oct 1867
Died Feb 1, 1930

Unknown

Mother
Minnie M. WYNFREY
Jan 16, 1900
June 4, 1969

Robert B. HERBERT
1900 - 1966

Hezzie L. WILSON Sr.
Apr. 19 1929
Apr. 27 1984

Alma C. KEYS
1878 - 1925

Pastor C. DABNEY
Born
Sept 1894
Died
Mar. 10, 1919

L. L. WYNNE
Born
July 16, 1869
Died
June 29, 1920

Lavina DABNEY
Born 1850
Died
May 10, 1923

John E.
BLACK
Born June 2, 1900
Died Dec. 18, 1927
The memory shall
ever be

A guiding star
to Heaven
Eva S. BYRDSONG
Born June 20, 1892
Died Dec. 26. 1928

Mother
Pauline D.
THORNTON
May 8, 1873
Dec. 17, 1936
Only asleep

Lawrence BLEWFORD
Born Dec. 14, 1902
Died May 13, 1942
Gone but not forgotten

Mrs. M. A. WYNNE
Born Dec. 8, 1869
Died Oct. 18, 1944

Horace WELL
1906 - 1968

Blanche WELLS
1899 - 1961

Mary E. JONES
1874 - 1964

Catherine W. DAVIS
1908 - 1974

J C CHRISTIAN
Born Feb 8 1868
Died Sept. 5 1949

George A. DAVIS
April 11, 1906
May 16, 1969

Mary P. DAVIS
Mar. 15 1907
Nov. 26, 1984

Crayer
Wife of
Sam
BAILEY
Died Sept. 8, 1927

Liza BROWN
1867 - 1918

Father
Mingo
PARKER
Aug. 1854
Jul. 5, 1921
Gone but not forgotten

Catherine W.
PARKER
Born
Nov. 14 1876
Died
Oct. 27 1943
Gone But not forgotten

Frederick Allen
MAYO
1957 - 1990

Unknown

Lucy
WASHINGTON
Born 1864
Died April 20 1945

Miles WYNNE
Born Oct 27 1851
Died Dec 2 1942

Eliza
Wife of
Miles
WYNNE
Died Feb. 7, 1928
age 70 yrs.
May the resurrection
find thee on the bosom of
thy God

Alexander SMITH
1895 - 1960

Bessie SMITH
Dec. 31, 1898
Mar. 24, 1982

Samuel TAYLOR
Died Sept. 13, 1945

Mrs. Josephine
TAYLOR
1878
Feb 6, 1950

Unknown

Tommie
son of
John & Hanna
HUDGINS
Born Feb 28, 1902
Died May 19, 1919

May the Resurrection
find thee
On the bosom of
thy God

Arthur
WILLIAM
Virginia
Pvt 446 Res
Labor Bn.
June 23, 1938

Father
Thomas C.
WILLIAM
Nov 16, 1866
Jun 16, 1926
AT REST

Custis EDWARDS
Sept. 22, 1915
April 12, 1989
d/s w/ Clara D.

Clara D. EDWARDS
May 13, 1914
June 10, 1988
d/s w/ Custis

Kissiah REED
Oct. 15, 1875
Nov. 10, 1970

Albert W. PEARSON Sr.
May 4 1916
Dec 5 1984

Wilbert TALTON
Born Sept 11 1908
Died Sept 7 1950

Cemeteries

Mother Granny
Marion T.
SMITH
Oct. 19, 1908
Jan. 14, 1992

Theodora M CHEVIONRS
Departed life
Aug 17 1935

A. T. BOOTH
Born Dec 11 1903
in New York City
Died Nov 3 1935

Earnest FRANCIS
Born Aug. 1, 1900
Died April 14, 1938

Maggie
wife of
Frank
JARVIS
Born May 12, 18??
Died Nov. 26, 1???
Grave where is
Thy victory ?

Henry JARVIS Sr.
March 11, 1860
March 15, 1944
d/s w/ Louise

Louise White JARVIS
Jan 10 1885
Dec. 24, 1935
d/s w/ Henry

Dorothy J. WHITE
Wife of W. H. WHITE
Born Feb. 11, 1911
Died Nov. 21, 1939

Samuel E.
MOORE

William H.
MOORE Sr.
PFC
U. S. Army
World War II
June 9 1926
Mar. 25 1990

Solomon A. MOORE Sr
July 9, 1896
Jan. 13, 1935
d/s w/ Louise Walker

Louise Walker MOORE
Aug. 18, 1900
Feb. 28, 1989

Harry W. Moore
Virginia CPL. Tank Co.
8 Cavalry Regt.
October 25, 1932
October 26, 1960

Harry S. MOORE
Nov. 3, 1957
July 26, 1987
(at bottom)
Franklin

Solomon A. MOORE
U. S. Army
World War II
1920 1978

Daniel CARY
Born Jan 1, 1887
Died Dec 29, 1937

Corinne CARY
May 19, 1889
Sept 20, 1979

James L. BOYD
U. S. Marine Corps
Oct. 4, 1947
Oct. 30 1987

Rosanna J. BOOKER
Died
Sept. 3, 1980

Unknown

Robert WALKER
1876 - 1964

William WALKER
1905 - 1965

James A. WALKER
April 26, 1901
Feb 2, 1983

JOHNSON
Freddie L.
1914 1967

My Mother
Rosa L. ALLEN
Died Dec. 22, 1939
Asleep in Jesus

John SCOTT
Born Jan 7, 1887
Died Apr. 8, 1927
Gone but not Forgotten

Eva L. EDLOW
March 14, 1915
June 28, 1986

Elizabeth L. TALTON
Oct. 17, 1924
May 31, 1987
"Wait on the Lord"
Psalms 27:14

Father
James TALTON
Nov. 10, 1875
Nov. 19, 1932
d/s w/ Eva V.

Mother
Eva V. TALTON
Oct. 12, 1892
Oct. 17, 1924

Bertha P. TALTON
Jan. 30, 1917
Oct. 14, 1987
d/s w/ Isaac E.

Isaac E. TALTON Sr.
Nov. 21, 1913
Oct. 14, 1987

Claude C. TALTON
Born Jan 20, 1910
Died May 24, 1961

Lelia Wynn JONES
Aug. 26, 1877
Mar. 10, 1965

Asia R. ROBERTS
Died April 3, 1959

Stanley TRUMBLE
Sept 4, 1951
Feb. 2, 1987

John TRUMBLE Sr.
May 21, 1914
May 19, 1978

Daisy M. BOYD
Aug. 4, 1910
Feb. 27, 1960

Willis HAYES, Sr.
1914 - 1974

Annie CHRISTIAN
Aug 29, 1907
July 23, 1975
From the children of
The Christian Family
in Memory of
Mrs. Annie M.
CHRISTIAN

Gracie HUGHES
Dec. 23, 1888
Oct. 2, 1975

Estherine COLEMAN
1925 -
d/s w/ Leroy

Leroy COLEMAN
1930 - 1978
d/s w/ Estherine

Isabella Farmer MOORE
Aug. 20 1900
Oct 25 1979
f/s

Alexander MOORE
1872 - 1944
f/s

Viola E. DIGGS
Born Oct. 6, 1926
Died June 10, 1931

Willie L. HOLMES
May 9, 1902
March 6, 1991

Estelle WILLIAMS
Mar. 9, 1917
Oct. 17, 1990

Sadie HOLMES
Born April 13, 1902
Died Dec. 16, 1951

Bertha E. JONES
March 9, 1907
August 3, 1987

Reuben EALEY, Sr.
Dec. 28, 1920
May 17, 1979

Robert E. FOX
May 1 1893
Jan 7 1971

Estelle Cary FOX
April 1908
Oct 8 1945

Josephine PARKER
Nov. 16, 1903
July 2 1980

George PARKER
Jan 25 1904
Aug 28 1983

Edna Parker WILLIAMS
Died Dec. 11 1968

Wilhelmina ELEY
1911 - 1958

ALLMOND
1977

Isaiah TRUMBLE, Jr.
March 3?, 1966
Oct. 18, 1987

NAZARETH
Juanita Stokes
13 Jan 1927
11 Sep 1990
In Loving Memory

Robert E. NAZARETH
1871 - 1946
d/s w/ Iadare L.

Iadare L. NAZARETH
1895 - 1958
d/s w/ Robert E.

Johnnie E.
NAZARETH
PFC
World War I
April 30 1897
August 4 1932

Chauncy V. NAZARETH
Jan 21 1918
June 3 1993
"Jack"

Robert H. NAZARETH
Sept 15 1918
Dec 30 1993

Dora Lee TAYLOR
Born Oct 7 1898
Died June 27 1942

Ambridge FOX
Died 1930

____ FOX
Born 1873
Died 1937

Jefferson A. FOX
Born 1912
Died 1941

SGT Milton L.
PARKER
1930 - 1950

Susan DIGGS
Born
March 1 1854
Died March 3 1942

Rest in Peace
Maggie DIGGS
Born 1897
Died 1952

Mrs. Victoria SMITH
Born May 9 1887
Died July 6 1953

Unknown

Walker
DABNEY
Virginia
Pvt 369 Infantry
93 Division
World War I
March 15 1894
May 26, 1950

Gladys BLOOK?
Born 1912
Died July 30 19?0

Barney E. WYNNE
Born Dec 30, 1886
Died Oct 28, 1950

J. H. BLACK
Born
Jan 1 1906
Died
Dec. 17 1944

Lawrence BLUEFORD,
Jr.
Oct 7, 1928
Apr. 8, 1956

Unknown

Winnie CHRISTIAN
May 29, 1908
Jan. 20, 1965

Erma COFER
Jan. 5, 1932
Jan. 9, 1971

Florence COFER
Dec. 2, 1914
April 13, 1978

Frederick A.
BOYKIN
Born July 2, 1929
Died Aug 16, 1945
Israel praised
thee O Lord with all
My Heart
At Rest

Naomi A. GAYLE
Sept. 7, 1930
Feb. 11, 1945

Cemeteries of the City of Newport News, formerly Warwick County, Virginia

Douglas
FRANCIS
Born May 8, 1898
Died May 26 1958

Lillian W. FRANCIS
Sept. 10, 1896
Nov. 19, 1967

Wyatt SPENCER
Oct. 17, 1911
July 10, 1993

Alexander E. SPENCER
Oct. 15, 1909
Jan. 16, 1993
(Elijah) on vault
d/s w/ Evelyn N.

Evelyn N. SPENCER
Dec. 6, 1922

Henry D. SPENCER
June 15, 1924
Dec. 26, 1988

Robert Wyatt SPENCER
Nov. 18, 1875
March 13, 1951
d/s w/ Patti Vivian

Patti Vivian Pointer
SPENCER
Jan. 25, 1887
Nov. 15, 1944

Mattie E. JOHNSON
Born Oct. 5, 1878
Died June 30, 1948

Martha OWENS
1880 - 1960

Arlethia
KEYES
May 12, 1925
Sept 19, 1954
Duvall
Rest in Peace

Moses Lester BANKS
Born Dec. 11, 1901
Died June 15, 1961

Ruth
TILLERY
Feb. 18, 1917
Nov. 26, 1983

Silas HUDSON
Aug 27, 1889
June 3, 1964

Unknown

John BLUEFORD
Born
May 2 (1?), 1892
Died
Date below ground

Henry Lee COMBS
Virginia
PFC COE, 388 Engineers
World War II
Dec 31, 1915   Dec 1, 1954

Rosetta B. COMBS
March 18, 1898
Feb 2, 1987

Walter LEEBA
Dec. 8, 1910
Nov. 23, 1980

Mary L. DIGGS
July 10, 1896
May 5, 1982

Earl D. JONES
May 24, 189?
May 11, 198?

Lenard T. WILLIAMS
Dec 17, 1887
Nov. 1, 1968

Adelia T. WILLIAMS
Sept 26, 1902
Aug 21, 1985

Watt
TALTON
Died Aug 14
A love one
from us
has gone

Delia TALTON
Sept. 18, 1870
Oct. 2, 1974

Rebecca COPELLAN
Born Feb 19, 1915
Died 1951

Solomon TALTON
Sgt US Army
World War II
1919   1988

Solomon HUDGINS
Nov. 6, 1900
Dec 12, 1982
Editha DODSON
April 3, 1904
April 28, 1964

Rosa WHITE
Died May 15, 1953
Age 52 Years

Spencer REED
1891 - 1963

Virginia T. DIGGS
Dec. 1, 1924
Sept. 16, 1964

Anthony SWANN
1876 - 1967

Estelle PHILLIPS
June 15, 1908
May 14, 1956

Samuel MARROW
Born Jan 2, 1892
Died March 21, 1955

Ellen THOMAS
Born Feb 8, 1880
Died Jan 1, 1935
Gone but not
forgotten

John THOMAS
1876 - 1957

Willie A. LEWIS, Jr.
July 14, 1931
March 29, 1968

William E. WARDEN
Aug. 14, 1886
April 3, 1971

Deborah L.
ROBINSON
SFC
US Army
Oct 11, 1956
Feb 11, 1993

Robert C. DOUGLAS
Aug. 16, 1908
Mar. 16, 1984

Arlene BANK
Oct. 1, 1903
Dec. 31, 1969

Son
Stanley
DAVIS, Jr.
June 21   Mar 29
1966   1883

Herbert MILLS
1884 Born N. C.
Oct 19, 1950
d/s w/ Maggie

Maggie MILLS
April 16, 1890
d/s w/ Herbert

Etta Diggs KIRBY
Aug 31, 1890
Aug 11, 1947
d/s w/ Benjamin H.
f/s E.D.K.

Benjamin H. KIRBY
June 9, 1892
Jan. 24, 1967
d/s w/ Etta Diggs
f/s B.H.K.

Vivian A. SPENCER
June 12, 1916
July 26, 1969

Melba C. STOKES
Oct. 29, 1920
Oct. 1, 1967

Roberta S. LICON
Aug. 15, 1905
Sept. 14, 1982

John Thomas LIGON
May 13, 1902
Sept. 20, 1982

Sarah Jane SPENCER
1924 - 1994

Patsey KEYES
July 24, 1897
July 27, 1967

Ellis H. TALTON
Feb. 18, 1903
Aug. 29, 1963

Alice Ida DIGGS
Oct. 5, 1898
Dec. 22, 1965

Seldon DIGGS
March 7, 1893
Dec. 1, 1968

Lena M. JEFFERSON
Feb. 8, 1919
Jan 29, 1992
on vault
Feb 8, 1918

Marjorie C. PERDY
Jan 11 1925
Nov 3 1957
on vault
Marjorie Clarice PERDY

Rechetta COMBS
Sept 12, 1893
July 15, 1955

Miss Clareave
SEAWARISHT
Born
Mar. 3, 1921
Died
Dec. 12, 1956

Jessie R. LANGFORD
Sept. 17, 1914
April 9, 1990

Ernest LANGFORD
April 3, 1902
April 27, 1988

Unknown

William H. ARRINGTON
1916 - 1967

Icah G. BARRANT
Aug. 31, 1907
Nov. 4, 1978

George W. JENNINGS
April 11, 1911
March 24, 1983

Jack H. KETCHMORE
AS US Navy
World War II
Oct 25 1919
Sept 19, 1983

Willie KETCHMORE
May 20 1915
May 8 1967

Virgie EDLOW
May 22, 1876
Dec 29, 1966

GONE TO BE AN
ANGEL
Theodore M.
BLAND, Jr.
March 21, 1975
March 27, 1981
WE LOVE YOU

Carrie GRAY
May 2, 1907
July 6, 1979
d/s w/ Clifton

Clifton GRAY
Mar 29, 1905
d/s w/ Carrie

Jeanette Esther BROWN
Sept 20, 1899
Sept. 7, 1966

Ann FERNANDES
Apr. 3, 1914
Nov. 20, 1978

Lillie SCOTT
June 3, 1897
Aug. 27, 1965

Helen W. BRIGGS
Sept. 20, 1943
Sept. 16, 1977

Ruth Cary HUNDLEY
June 2, 1923
Oct. 31, 1973

Josephine W. REED
1911 -- 1964
f/s Mother

Arthur REED
Jan. 27, 1891
July 10, 1964

Alma O. WILLIAMS
Sept. 18, 1937
Jan. 18, 1985

Irene P.
PARKER
March 26, 1903
March 17, 1993

Henrietta G. M. BAKER
1898 -- 1957

Nelson PARKER
Oct 27, 1894

William M. PARKER
March 6, 1901
Oct 17, 1958
Beloved Husband

Edward M.
PARKER
PVT
US Army
April 6, 1924
Sept. 22, 1983

Mary L. PARKER
Aug. 8, 1928
Oct. 28, 1982

Jacqueline
TAYLOR
1992

Fernando FRANCIS
1992

Steven CHAPMAN
March 18, 1993
small grave

Joanna CHAPMAN
March 6, 1992
small grave

Icah Keith BARRANT
Jan. 15, 1955
May 25, 1984

Ernest COMBS
Dec. 15, 1901
June 11, 1984

Helen T. COMBS
Feb. 20, 1902
Nov. 22, 1987

Samuel L. JARVIS
Aug. 22, 1947
April 17, 1990

Unknown

Annie B. SHIELDS
Oct. 23, 1902
Feb. 26, 1968

Clifton ROBINSON
Oct. 12, 1909
Oct. 6, 1962

Christopher THOMAS
Dec. 25, 1871
Feb. 12, 1963

Mattie THOMAS
Oct 6, 1964

Alberta THOMAS
Aug 25 1902
June 6 1982

OLD SECTION

Edward DIGGS
Born 1843
Aged 72 Years
Private U. S. 1 colored
G No. 36 Company

Mary
wife of
Sam JONES
died Dec. 31, 1924
Age 60 years
Gone but not forgotten

A. W. POOLE
Sergeant 36th Regt
Company G. U.S.
Colored Troops
Born August 30th 1845
Died Sept. 12th 1912
f/s A.W.P.

L. J. BANKS
Born June 3, 1888
Died June 10 1901

Anthony M. POOLE
Born
June 3, 1885
Died
Feb. 5, 1892

Lugie A. NELSON
Born
April 27 1899
Died
March 16 1906

Lucy F. POOLE
Born
April 17, 1864
Died
Nov. 27, 1907

J. N. SPRATLEY
Died August 1, 1913
aged 60 years
Gone but not forgotten

Rosanna SPRATLEY
Born
June 19 1861
Died
June 15 1882

Father
Richard SMITH
Mother
Henrietta SMITH
f/s R.S. & H. S.

Mother
Bertie NAZARETH
Born 1854
April 17 1926
At rest

George W. ALLMOND
Born March 15 1872
Died May 25 1921

Fannie WALKER
Born Feb. 22 1849
Died Dec. 15 1916

William B. WALKER
? 2 1844
Died Sept. 2? 1885
At Rest

William A.
WILLIAMS
Born March 29, 1868
Died March 25. 40

(Left Side)
Sara SMITH
Died
May 26, 1919
(Front)
Aaron SMITH
Died
Aug 3, 1925
Millie SMITH
Died
March 8, 1929

(Right Side)
William SMITH
Died
Oct. 10, 1880
f/s S.S., M.S., A.S., W.S.

Robert Henry
NAZARETH
Born Aug. 12, 1848
Died
Aug 25, 1914

Barney DABNEY
Died
Aug 27, 1911
Aged 60 years

Agnes REECE

W. T. Reece
Born Mar 31, 1867
Died Mar 30, 1923
Mother
Agnes REECE
Born June 10, 1841
Died April 16, 1895
(Other Side of Stone)
Nettie REECE
Age 1 Year
Moses REECE
Age 2 Years
f/s W.T.H.

Annie CARY
Died
July 3, 1911
Aged 45 Years

Father
Piant
LIPFORD
Apr 28 1882
Jun 7 1928
Gone but not
forgotten

Edward
LIPFORD
1800 - 1918
At Rest

Flottie Bertha
Daughter of
J. and Emma D.
JOHNSON
Born Oct 14 1906
Died Sep 3 1908

Jerry THOMAS
Died
Feb 3, 1910
Aged 80 Years

Adline MOODY
Died April 10, 1908
At Rest

Mrs Susian BLACK
July 28, 1852
July 28 1913
Aged 60 Years
Asleep in Jesus
peaceful rest

J. M. JONES
Born
Sept. 1, 1857
Died May 2 1914

Mary
Wife of
Jerry THOMAS
Died Apr. 14, 1821
Aged 85 Yrs.
Gone but not forgotten

Pattie BUTTS
Oct 29, 1887
Oct 16, 1905
Asleep in Jesus
Knights of Gideon No. 23

Hariet Anna
BUTTS
Died Feb 1920
Aged 32 Years
f/s H.A.B.

Peter MOODEY
Died
June 20, 1910
Aged 76 Years
f/s P.Mo.

H. H. ROSS
Born
Jan 25, 1937
Died
Nov 17, 1907

Adline ROSS
Died
Nov 21, 1906
Age 69 Years

Albert FIELDS
Born Dec 17, 1877
Died Apr 2, 1924

Emma
Wife of
Willie MARROW
Died Jan 6, 1923 Age 45
years
As a wife devoted
as a mother affectionate
as a friend
ever kind and true.

Ed. JOINS
Born 1861 Died 1919

Mother
Fanny JOINS
--ed March 24, 182-
--e but n-- - -orgotten

Unknown

f/s E. L.

1st Baptist Church Denbigh Cemetery

1st Baptist Church Denbigh Cemetery

Acknowledgment: Transcribed by Frank Hutchinson's Boy Scout Troop # 108, done by Scouts toward their Eagle Scout Badge, and researched by Gertrude Stead.

BENN'S ROAD CEMETERY
BENNS ROAD (11) {I 11}

The cemetery is a small fenced in area with no gate. There are only three flat tombstones, It is not certain they are lying in the proper places. Two of the stones are broken. We have been unable to find any background on this cemetery.

The transcription are:

John C. MARROW	Samuel Seldner	(Name broker off)
Son of W. C. MARROW	GROOME	(Mary A. T.)
& Mary A. T. MARROW	Died May 15, 1879	wife of Wm. C. MARROW
Departed this life	Age 10 month	Born
April 4, 1855		Apr. 20, 1809
In his 25th year of his age		Died
		Feb. 28, 1885

	From the Certification of Death of Samuel S. Groome	Mary T. Marrow;
Place of Death	Warwick Co. Va.	Warwick Co. Va.
Line Number	16	48
Name of Deceased	Saml. S. Groome	Mary T. Marrow
Race	White	White
Sex	Male	Female
Age	12 Months	76 yr 3 mo 4 da
Date of Death	May 20, 1879	February 28, 1884
Place	Warwick Co. Va.	Morrisons
Cause of Death	Not Stated	Pneumonia
Name of Parents	C. F. Groome & Emma	Not Stated
Birthplace of Deceased	Warwick	Elizabeth City
Occupation	Not Stated	housekeeper
Consort of	Not Stated	Not Stated
Name of Informant	C. F. Groome	Edwin Phillips
Relation of Informant	Father	Not Stated
Commissioner of the Revenue	W. C. Marrow	M. D. Wright
Date Record Filed	August 1880	Between 1884 & 1896

St. Paul's Episcopal Church, 221 - 34th Street, Newport News, Va. has in their burial records- "1885 - Mary Wife of W. C. Morrow - Home *Morrison* called *Oakville*"

Slab type stone of John C. Marrow

Slab type stone of (Mary A. T. Marrow)

Acknowledgment: Researched, transcribed and photographed by Gertrude Stead.

BLOOMING BAPTIST CHURCH
AFRICAN AMERICAN
OYSTER POINT ROAD (4) {l 24}

The following inscriptions were taken from the tombstones in the church cemetery. There are only two tombstones in this cemetery, but there are about 25 other burials in this cemetery. This African-American Church was founded in 1896.

Mother
Bessie SMITH
Born
Aug. 15, 1876
Died July 17, 1925
Sleep on dear mother
and take thy rest

Dear Husband
J. H. MONTAGUE
Born Apr. 8, 1886
Glouster Co., Va.
Died - July 23
1933 *Gone but*
not forgotten
Dear Husband
Sleep on and
take thy rest

Blooming Baptist Church Cemetery

Tombstone of J. H. MONTAGUE

Acknowledgment: Researched, inventoried and photographed by Gertrude Stead.

CARY BURYING GROUND
"PEARTREE HALL"

TABBS LANE and RAYMOND DRIVE (22) {I 19}

The following is from the *Virginia Historical Inventory, (W P A), The Library of Virginia.*

"The description of this burying ground in 1937:
The Cary burying ground at "Peartree Hall" is quite large. It is surrounded by an iron fence, which has written on the gate, "Barnes of Richmond, 1840". The real old tombstones in the graveyard have been destroyed; however, there are two slab and two monument markers of a later date. Some graves are not marked at all. There are several trees in the graveyard, and some underbrush. In the spring, when the jonquils are blooming, the place is a solid mass of yellow, a beautiful sight. Today, there has been a house built on this property, with a high wooden fence so the graves are not visible."

The following inscriptions were copied from the tombstones: 1937

Sarah E. S.
Daughter of
Col. James BAY-TOP
and
Wife of
Col. Gill Armistead CARY
Born Sept. 18, 1790
Died April 15, 1879

Susan CARY
Daughter of
Col. John CARY
of
Elizabeth City
County
Born Sept. 27, 1789
Died March 1873

Gill A. CARY
Son of
John & Susannah CARY
Born March 18th 1783
Died March 25th 1843
"*Mark the perfect man
Behold the upright
For the end of the man
is peace.*"

John B. CARY, Junr.
Son of
John B. & Columbia CARY
Born November 25th 1846
Died August 10th 1860
"*Whosoever therefore shall
confess me before men, him
will I confess also before
my Father which is in heaven.*"

There is much history associated with "Peartree Hall," the following is from the *Denbigh Gazette* March 31, 1993.

"The Cary's Peartree Hall Plantation stood in the heart of Denbigh way into the 20th Century. The home, built by Miles Carey, Jr. and originally called "Potash Creek," was the home of many distinguished Cary's including Judge Richard Cary, stood at the end of present day Tabbs Lane. Lore says that present day Tabbs Lane was the road which lead to Peartree Hall. A reference was found which alluded to the fact that Peartree stood at the end of "Cary's Lane" and later the road was referred to as Peartree Lane. After the Tabbs took over the estate from the Campbells it was referred to and later officially named Tabbs Lane.

The manor was a two and a half story structure made of both brick and wood. Double entrance doors were on the first and second story which opened onto verandas which ran the length of the house. For the times it was quite a showplace. There were several outbuildings including a large kitchen used to prepare food and meals for the retinue of the plantation. A kitchen as an outbuilding was common in colonial days as fires were frequent in kitchens and could easily be contained in an outbuilding away from the main house out of harms way in the event of fire.

Judge Richard Cary besides being a tobacco planter was also a botanist somewhat in the image of his northern neighbor, Thomas Jefferson, would be some years later. He supervised his work force in constructing terraced gardens which were referred to as "botanical gardens". Cary exchanged species with other botanists in England and France. Old time Denbigh residents can recall vestiges of these terraces behind the present day Lowe's store (1996 MCI) as well as periwinkles and assorted daffodils and tulips growing wild in the woods surrounding the estate. Cary's major crop was like all tidewater growers, tobacco. Cary did sacrifice much of his potential crop by using many acres for his gardens.

Richard Cary's wife was Mary Cole of nearby Bolthrope Plantation located a mile or so away on the shore of the Warwick River just off the intersection of present day Moyer Road and Beechmont Drive. Cary himself was quite affluent, he was Sheriff, clerk of courts, an officer in the militia and a judge. Surviving records from the 1810 courthouse has his name affixed to documents in one or more of the positions that he held in the county.

While Wilson Cary was owner of the estate, he had a charming young daughter named Mary Cary. Mary was a beauty and turned every bachelor's head in the surrounding counties. One of her suitors was a young aspiring Virginian named Washington, George Washington to be exact. George paid court to Miss Mary Cary and he called on her at Peartree Plantation.

So George Washington the father of Our Country did trod in Denbigh and possibly spent several nights or more as a guest of the Wilson Cary's. George was well off at the time, however Wilson Cary just did not take a liking to him at all. In fact he conveyed to Mary that she already had a coach of her very own to ride in and certainly did not need his.

All this came to an end one evening at nearby Carter's Grove in the now infamous "Refusal Room", where according to lore, Mary Cary told George, "No!" to his proposal of marriage. Mary later married Jacqueline Ambler, Jacquline being the poor fellow's mother's maiden name that he was stuck with for life. Ambler built on Jamestown Island and the walls of the manor house, reinforced by the efforts of our National Park Service, still stand today.

The house passed out of the Cary direct lineage to the Lucas family, then Campbells and finally the Tabbs. The house did survive British random ransacking of plantations such as took place at Captain Samuel Mathew's Denbigh Plantation during the Revolutionary War and again in the War of 1812.

The Cary grave yard was at one time very extensive. At one time there were over 30 marked graves all enclosed by a wrought iron fence. Two old time Denbigh residents have informed me that the same fate that befell the graves at nearby Potters Field also befell the majority of graves at the Cary site. They were developed over with no regards to history or the sanctity of the grave. Only a few graves survive today as the picture shows. There are a few chunks of remaining headstones and vestiges of a linked grouping of graves. The property was later sold to the Denbigh Baptist Church. The church rented the land to a farmer from Gloucester. The farmer removed the wrought iron fence from the grave yard and moved it to his place in Gloucester.

Although Peartree Hall survived the British raiding party that sacked part of Denbigh in the War of 1812, it did not fare too well during the Civil War. No, it wasn't the Yankees who did the damage, but the locals. Before the war, Peartree Hall had, as stated two story verandas in front and rear of the home. During the war, with the residents gone, these porches were dismantled for firewood. After the war when it was preoccupied by its owners steps were made to the first floor doors but the second story door to the porch in both front and rear led to a ten foot drop. Money was scarce then and the land was just about farmed out from improper rotation of fields, fertilization and plain neglect. People made do with what they had to survive.

The final occupants of Peartree Hall were two old maid sisters, Misses Edith and Fannie Tabb. The girls got on in their dotage and were a tad bit on the senile side. A visitor might be informed that they had just missed seeing Governor Pollard who was the Governor of Virginia at the time. Or another time it would be Senator Byrd, or Congressman so and so.

After the Tabb sisters passed away, their will passed the property on to the Denbigh Baptist Church. The church rented the land to a farmer from Gloucester. The farmer removed the wrought iron fence from the grave yard and moved it to his place in Gloucester.

This gave impetus to the desecration of the grave yard as vandals took their toll on the markers by breaking them or stealing the markers and placing them in peoples front yards as a joke.

When the farmer quit renting the land, the Denbigh Baptist Church sold the property to developers and the rest is history. Peartree Hall was razed in the early 50's or so and thus ended another chapter of Denbigh history."

From the *Daily Press,* Newport News, Va. May 12, 1994:
"The article is in reference to the destruction of the cemetery by a developer. In the article it brings to attention that Judge Richard Cary, represented Warwick in the convention that drafted the state's 1776 constitution, is buried there."

Today, 1997, a house has been built on this property and a high wooden fence is around the backyard, so you cannot see the graves.

Acknowledgment: Gertrude Stead, research, photographs and transcribing remaining graves.

Carey Burying Ground "Peartree Hall"

CEMETERIES DESTROYED, MOVED, NOT FOUND, OR ACCESS DENIED

1ST BAPTIST CHURCH MORRISON CEMETERY

JANMAR DRIVE (2) {I 30}

The church denied the Tidewater Genealogy Society permission to transcribe tombstone in the church cemetery.

CAMP BUTLER FEDERAL PRISON CAMP CONFEDERATE

PRESENT DAY C & O PROPERTY (37) {G 51}

The Confederate Soldiers buried at Camp Butler, near the end of the Civil War were removed to Greenlawn Cemetery on Shell Road. Greenlawn Cemetery is partly in the City of Newport News and partly in the City of Hampton. The names of the Confederate Soldiers can be found in the *Elizabeth City County / City of Hampton Tombstone Inscriptions*.

CONFEDERATE GRAVEYARD SITE

JEFFERSON AVENUE (YODER FARM) (27) {M 22}

The following is from the *Virginia Historical Inventory, (W P A), The Library of Virginia*. Information acquired 1937.

"Location:
    One and one half miles east of Denbigh, on Route #517; thence one and seven tenths miles south on Jefferson Avenue Extension Highway. (Do not know number) directly on highway, east side.

Date:
    1861

Owners:
Mirandi Walls, (original)	1861 - 1866
Solomon Reeser,	1866 - 1898
J. F. Hebbard,	1898 - 1898
Magruder B. Jones,	1898 - 1898
D. S. Yoder	1898 - 1936
Heirs of D. S. Yoder, (Present)	1936 -

Description:
   There is no evidence today of there once being a graveyard. The site is situated in an open field. A road runs across one part of the graveyard.

Historical Significance:
   This confederate graveyard was not far distant from the camping ground of the soldiers during the War Between the States. So many died from hunger and disease. It was not know by many that there was a graveyard in this spot. Around three years ago, when the new Jefferson Avenue Extension Highway was built, it was run across this graveyard and some skeletons were plowed up.

   This confederate Graveyard has been sold along with the "Old Walls' estate" each time it has been conveyed.

Informant:
   Mrs. Harvey Yoder, Oyster Point, Virginia. whose husband is present owner."

The site in 1997 is about the interchange of Jefferson Avenue and Interstate 64.

GIBBS' FAMILY GRAVEYARD

RICHNECK ROAD (WATERWORKS PROPERTY) (17) {P 13}

The following information is from the *Virginia Historical Inventory, (W P A), The Library of Virginia*. Information acquired in 1937.

"Owners:
   Gibbs family, original owners.
   Newport News Water company, present owners.

Description:
   The Gibbs' family graveyard is situated about one mile from the main road in the woods. It is on a high bluff overlooking a little creek. Lovely old beech trees are growing all around the graveyard. There are no tombstones. This graveyard is almost forgotten.

Informant:
Mr. Leonard Fowler, Denbigh, Va."

HUNTINGTON HEIGHTS

SEE NEWPORT NEWS FARMS (39) {H 43}

CEMETERIES ON NEWPORT NEWS FARMS

   The following family cemeteries are from the articles "*The Old Farms out of which the City of Newport News was Erected*" by W. T. Stauffer. These articles were first published in the *William and Mary Quarterly, Series two, Volumes 14 and 15 in 1934.*
   The articles were reprinted in the *Virginia Tidewater Genealogy Quarterly, Volumes 23, Number 4, 1992; volume 24, Number 1 and 2, 1993; Volume 25, Number 1, 2 and 4, 1994 and Volume 26, Number 1 and 2, 1995.*

"William LEE Homestead: Now Huntington Heights Area: There was a burying ground on Sixty Fifth Street about 200 feet from Huntington Avenue. Skeletons were found when digging foundations for houses at 314, 313 and 316 - 65th Street. No mention is made if these bodies were interred in other cemeteries.

HAWKINS Farm: The Hawkins Family Cemetery was located 150 feet west of West Avenue and 70 feet north of Thirty First Street. The bodies were later moved to the Hawkins lot in Greenlawn Cemetery.

WILBERN Farm: The Wilbern family burying ground was just south of Thirtieth Street on the bluff. The bodies were removed but the article does not state to where they were moved.

John PARRISH Farm: The Parrish farm was located near the Ivy Avenue pier, east of Madison Avenue and extending back from Hampton Roads. There were no tombstones above ground.

BURK Farm: There were two burying grounds on this land. One within the old Dodge Plant land on what is now Orcutt Avenue. Before World War I, grave mounds and old stones without inscriptions were still seen. Edward T. Ivy had these bodies moved to Greenlawn Cemetery. The other graveyard was move, was a public burying ground and used by both white and Negroes (African Americans). Twenty-first Street, between Madison and Marshall Avenue runs through this burial site. There is nothing left to indicate that it was the burial site of human beings.

Wilson Miles CARY: In a deed to David Brodie, Wilson Miles Cary reserved a burying ground at a place on "Celey" called "Cherry Grove". The grave site was located at what is the Northwestern corner of Kecoughtan Road and Sycamore Avenue. (This land was annexed by City of Newport News in 1927.)

James BURKS: Two burial grounds were on this property. One was a public graveyard said to be for poor whites, Negroes and Indians. This site was located near the mouth of Salters Creek, not far from the bridge where the Boulevard street car line crossed Salter's Creek. The Federal Government removed these bodies when it made this area part of Camp Stuart (World War I). The Burks' graveyard was on the bluff, about 200 feet east of where Roanoke Avenue extended would reach the bluff. (Camp Stuart land was originally part of Elizabeth City County and later Warwick County. It was annexed into Newport News in 1940).

NEW APOSTOLIC CHURCH CEMETERY

WARWICK BOULEVARD (35) {j 16}

This cemetery is located next to the Potter's Field Cemetery. There are approximately 14 to 16 graves in this cemetery.

NORTH BRICKYARD ROAD CEMETERY

MIDDLESEX DRIVE (TODAY) (32) {K 30}

This cemetery has not been located to date, but graves were known to be on Middlesex Drive about 30 years ago.

OYSTER POINT ROAD CEMETERY

OYSTER POINT ROAD (31) {L 24}

This cemetery, family name is not known, was located near the railroad tracks. Graves were removed to Hampton Memorial Cemetery.

POTTER'S FIELD

WARWICK BOULEVARD (35) {J 16}

The property was purchased by Warwick County, November 15, 1893, and transferred to Newport News February 24, 1896. Information on this site can be found at *The Virginia State Library* in the records of *Newport News City Council, Committee No. 1,"Alms House and Poor"* and the *Warwick County Board of Supervisions papers from 1900 - 1935*. Buried on the site were 500 individuals. None of the graves are marked, but paupers were identified by name. Most interments were handled by W. J. Smith, Jr., Funeral Home on Harpersville Road. The last person to be buried in this cemetery was Mary Carey in March 1961.

RUSSELL GRAVEYARD

J. CLYDE MORRIS BLVD. AND OLD OYSTER POINT RD. (26) {P 28}

The following is from the *Virginia Historical Inventory, (W P A), The Library of Virginia*. Transcribed in January 11, 1937, recorded by Dorothy Diffenderfer

The Russell graveyard lies in a beautiful grove of ancient walnut trees. It is grown up in grass and underbrush. the graves are very hard to find. there are several small cedar markers, which have almost rotted away. Some of the graves are not marked at all. There are two large. flat slabs, which were cracked, but which were remodelled recently.

The following inscriptions were copied from the tombstones:

In
Memory of
Col. Thomas C. RUSSELL
of Rose-down, York County, Virginia,
Born Jany 4th 1793
Died Dec. 2nd 1851
Few men have lived and died more beloved and respect-
ed. The nobleness and generosity of his nature, the
purity and elevation of His character. The warmth and
disinterestedness of his friendships were acknowledged
and Admired by all who knew him. His friends were nu-
merous and devoted. Two of them have Caused this monu-
ment to be erected in testimony of their regards and
in commemoration of the virtues which adorned his life.

To My Husband
Edward S. RUSSELL
born Dec. 22nd 1811
Died May 8th 1858

This burial site has not been located in the 1990's.

SARAH B. WATSON GRAVE

WARWICK BOULEVARD (34) {I 40}

The following information comes from the "*The Times-Herald*" Aug. 7, 1942. "Military Camp Bears Woman's Name" - Pfc. Mallam is attached to a military police battalion encamped in Warwick County. Soldiers setting up the camp found the grave of Mrs. Sarah B. Watson, a Newport News resident during the War Between the States, and intimately associated with a leading local family of the period. Passing over military leaders, the commanding officer decided to name the camp in honor of Mrs. Watson. The newspaper article has a picture of Mrs. Watson's tombstone.

The reference to the leading local family of the area, was the West Family. More details of the life of Mrs. Sarah B. Watson can be found in Parke Rouse "The Day the Yankee Came" which gives a detailed history of Newport News Point and the West family during the Civil War. Mrs. Watson was married three times before she was 21 years old. After marrying her third husband she moved to Missouri, but she returned back to Virginia about 1841. It is believed that she was a friend of the West family before she went to Missouri. When she returned with $1500, she struck a bargain with the West family and lived and raised their children for the rest of her life. George Benjamin West had the Tombstone put in place some years after her death. It is believed that Mr George Ben West knew that her marriage was not a happy one and chose to put her parents on the tombstone.

In Memory
of
Mrs. Sarah B. WATSON
Daughter of
Saml. & Judith SKINNER
Born August 22, 1794
Died September 10, 1868

The Grave and tombstone have been moved to Richmond, we do not have the date when the grave was moved. It location was on Virginia Avenue today's Warwick Boulevard across from Huntington Park."

Acknowledgment: Gertrude Stead for researching and collecting information. The *Times-Herald* for the article 7 August 1942.

WALLS' SLAVE GRAVEYARD

PATRICK HENRY SHOPPING CENTER (25) {N 23}

The following is from the *Virginia Historical Inventory, (W P A), The Library of Virginia.* Research made by Dorothy Diffenderfer, Denbigh, Virginia, August 27, 1937.

"Subject: Site of Walls' Slave Graveyard.

Location: 2.3 miles south of Denbigh, Virginia, on Route #60, thence 1 mile east on Route #2, thence 0.1 of a mile north on Jefferson Avenue road, thence 0.2 of a mile east on private road.

Date: Prior to 1860.

Owners: See report on D. S. Yoder's home. See below.

Description: The site of this graveyard is in a field. No tombstones were ever placed over the graves.

Historical Significance: These slaves belonged to Mirandi Walls, who owned a big plantation before the War Between the States.

Informant: Mrs. L. Glick, Oyster Point, Va.

The above information is from the *Virginia Historical Inventory (W P A), The Library of Virginia.*

Subject: D. S. Yoder Home

Location: 2.3 miles south of Denbigh, Virginia, on route #60, .08 miles east on Route #2. .1 mile north on Jefferson Avenue Highway (could not find number). .1 mile east on private road.

Date: Date unknown.

Owners: Warwick County records were destroyed during the War Between the States, therefore it is difficult to trace ownerships and dates of property.
Mirandi Walls ----1866
Jacob C. Shapp)
Soloman Reeser)   1866 - 1898

Christian Shapp)
John W. Klim)

J. F. Hubbard ------1898
M. B. Jones, September, 1898 -- December, 1898.
D. S. Yoder -----1898 - 1936
Heirs of D. S. Yoder – present owners.

Description:

The Yoder home is an old farmhouse which has been rebuilt and changed a great deal.

It is a large rectangular, two-story frame house. Originally there were three stories, the basement floor being the first story. The roof is gabled. There are three small chimneys-- not the original ones. The old fireplace chimneys were torn down. The chimneys there today are located on each end of the house, and one toward the center of the north side. There is a two-story screened porch on the south side of the house. There were originally three large porches. An outside stairway was built just outside of the porch. The front entrance is a plain four paneled door.

On the first floor are three rooms and a kitchen built on the north side in recent years. The big hall is used as a room. On the ceiling of the room on the west side is a beautifully decorated ring of flower in the center, made of plaster. A dark narrow box stairway leads from the middle room or hall upstairs where there are four rooms and a small screened porch. The old flooring is still in the house. The planks are wide varying in width. The woodwork is the original. The old doors are the four paneled type which are painted. The old house has been changed from its original arrangement to allow for a modern heating system.

Historical Significance:

When this house belonged to the "Wall Estate" it was a large beautiful home. At that time it had three stories. Each floor had a large hall with one big room on each side. There was a beautiful winding stairway which ran up though all the halls. Two huge fireplace chimneys ran up the ends of the house. There was a fireplace in each room. The house had three large verandas.

It is not known how many years before the War Between the States, Mirandi Walls owned the place. But he did have a handsome estate and owned over a hundred slaves. It is told that the Negroes used to steal things in the surrounding community, and take them to Walls, who would always give them money for their stolen goods. He was unusually good to all his slaves.

The Walls home was the center of big social gatherings. When the War Between the States came, the Walls family had to evacuate. The house was occupied by soldiers and the 10th, 8th, 6th, Alabama regiments and the 6th Georgia regiment were camped on the farm. A small fort was built by them just north of the house. It has been removed in recent years. Also there is a site of a Confederate graveyard near the house. After the War, on the porch columns were found initials of soldiers and dates carved in the wood.

In 1866, Mirandi Walls sold the home and farm of 1100 acres to Jacob C. Shapp, Soloman Reeser, Christian Shapp and John W. Klim. In 1897, the property was found in Chancery Court, and in 1898, J. F. Hubbard, Commissioner sold it the same year to Magruder B. Jones for $2,300. December 24, 1898, Jones sold the farm to D. S. Yoder for $3,700. He owned it until his death in 1936, when his heirs became the present owners."

There is an architectural description of the building in this Works Progress Administration records, it is not recorded in this book, because the subject matter is not relative.

Acknowledgment: Gertrude Stead for her research on the Walls' Slave Cemetery.

WILSON FAMILY GRAVEYARD

DEEP CREEK ROAD (28) {G 26}

This cemetery has not been located by the Tidewater Genealogical Society Researchers. The following is from the *Virginia Historical Inventory, (W P A), The Library of Virginia.*

"Location:
   4.3 miles south of Denbigh, Virginia, on route # 60; thence 1.3 miles west on Deep Creek Road; thence 0.1 of a mile on private road; thence 0.3 of a mile west on private road; thence 1 mile north on private road.

Owners:
   Wilson family, original,
   Z. R. Parker,
   John R. Parker, 1859-1901.
   J. E. Parker, present owner, from 1901.

Description:
   This old Wilson family graveyard is situated on a hill, very near the old house. There are a few trees standing. There are no tombstones in the graveyard; but the graves may be seen. It is grown up in weeds and grass.

Source of Information:
   Informant; Mr. J. E. Parker, Hilton Village, Va."

Acknowledgment: Gertrude Stead for research.

COLE FAMILY GRAVEYARD

PATRICK LANE (19) {G 13}

The following is from the *Virginia Historical Inventory, (W P A), The Virginia State Library. The William and Mary Quarterly Vol. 14, Series 1*, pages 165 and 166.

1937:
The Cole family burying ground is situated in a beautiful grove of old walnut trees near the site of the house. The graveyard is not taken care of. It is grown up in weeds and underbrush. The tombstones are very hard to find because they lie flat on the ground, beneath the underbrush. There is one whole tombstone, the one of William Cole. It has the Cole coat of arms. There are two other slabs, pieces of which have been lost.

HISTORICAL SIGNIFICANCE:
From the tombstone of William Cole you can get an idea of his life. A large piece, the length of the slab, has been broken off the stone of William Cole's daughter. Before the piece was broken off it read as follows:

"Here lyeth the Body of Martha, the Daughter of William COLE
and Martha His wife (daughter of John LEAR, Esq). Shee departed
this life the 19th day of April 1698, in ye eight year of her age o

Near also to this place lyeth the body of John COLE and Mary COLE,
two children of the said William and Martha".

The other tombstone is the marker of William COLE's wife. Before it was broken in many pieces, it read:

"Here lyeth the Body of Ann, the Wife of William COLE of
Warwick County, Esq. one of the daughters of Edward DIGGES, Esq.
son of Sir Dudley DIGGES, Master of the Rolls to King Charles the First.

She departed this life the 22nd day of November, 1658 in the
29th year of her age. Near also to this place lyeth the Bodys of
Edward COLE and Digges COLE, two Children of said Ann"

TRADITION:
Some years ago, a few ignorant boys of Warwick got the idea that Old King Cole (of the nursery rhymes) was buried in this grave yard. So they started digging, thinking they would find some of King's jewelry and gold. But, of course, all of this work was in vain because the King was never buried there or anywhere.

Here lyeth the Body of William COLE
Esq. of the County of Warwick who
departed this life the 4th day of March
1694 in the 56 year of His Age
There does not need this Marble to proclaim
His worth nor to immortalize his Name
His virtuous arts are of a Salling date
Family recorded in the Book of fate
Devouring time that not his glories Blot
Nor can (this age) his memory be-forgot
virtuous and industrious Life he lead
To all that would in Honest footsteps Tread
He was in All His Stations fair & greate
And stood as firm a pillar of the State
Of him May this be loudly sounded for
He was unspotted on ye bench
Untaynted at the bar

Here Lyeth the Body of
Daughter of William COLE
His wife (daughter of John LEAR)
Shee departed this life the 19th
April 1698 in ye eighth year

Near this place lyeth
John COLE & Mary COLE two chil

22nd Day
22nd Year
Also to this
Bodys of Edward
nd Digges COLE Two
ldren of the Said Ann

Here lyeth the Body
Wife of William COLE

Acknowledgment: Gertrude Stead, for research material and photographs of the site.

William Cole tombstone with Cole Coat of Arms

Broken slab tombstone of the Cole family

CURTIS CEMETERY
SUSAN CONSTANT ROAD (20) {J 14}

Curtis Cemetery

Tombstone of Miles G. Curtis

Tombstone of Daniel C. Patrick, C. S. A.

Martha J. Charles, wife of E. C. Charles, 1813 - 1890

Today the Curtis Cemetery is off Warwick Boulevard on Susan Constant Road, between Denbigh and Stoney Brook. In 1936 the following information was given in the W P A Records.

"Location: 0.9 of a mile north of Warwick Court House, Virginia, on Route 60, 0.3 of a mile west on private road, fifty yards south.

Date: 1844, date of oldest grave.

Owner: Descendants of Thomas Curtis.

Description: The Curtis Family Burying Ground is large. Some of the old tombstones were destroyed during the War Between the States. There are many markers of a more recent date. A chain of earthworks runs along the south side of the cemetery. The graveyard is kept in fair condition."

Historical Significance: The following inscription were copied from the tombstone;

W. H. CURTIS
Born
Feb. 2, 1827
Died
Sept. 1903
"As a father devoted
As a father affectionate
As a friend
Ever kind and true
In life he exhibited all
The grace of a Christian"

B. G. CURTIS, Jr.
Born
Dec. 19, 1863
Died
Aug. 27, 1872
Free from all temptation
No more need of watchful
care

E. G. CHARLES
Born
Oct. 19, 1818
Died
May 2, 1890

Sam'l G. CURTIS
Son of
Thos. CURTIS & Ann
His wife
Born April 12, 1823
Died Nov. 16, 1869
Age 73 years 7 mo 4 days

D. H. CURTIS
Born
May 25, 1852
Died
April 11, 1900
"Those who knew him
Best loved him most"

Martha
Harwood
CURTIS
April 3, 1836
March 4, 1911
Gone but not forgotten

Martha J.
wife of
E. C. CHARLES
Born
Nov. 25, 1813
Died
Jan. 22, 1890

Lewis P. CHARLES
Born
Oct. 17, 1852
Died
Dec. 27, 1907
Aged 55 years

In memory of
Our Mother
Ann D. GARROW
Born
March 14, 1818
Died
July 27, 1897
Aged 79 years
4 mo. & 13 das.
"Farewell and yet
Oh! not farewell
That word brings
Anguish to the brest
We Weep for thee
But know that thou
Art now at rest

Mother
Virginia Curtis
GARROW
Wife of John L. CURTIS
May 29, 1853
Dec. 22, 1930
"Asleep in Jesus
Blessed Sleep"

John T. GARROW
Born Aug. 15, 1820
Died Mar. 19, 1866

In Memory of
Martha T. GARROW
Born
March 20, 1859
Died
May 24, 1860

John J. GARROW
Born
June 30, 1846
Died
Feb. 25, 1860

In Memory of
Martha A. GARROW
Born
June 8, 1842
Died
Sept. 1, 1844

In Memory of
William H. GARROW
Born
July 14, 1840
Died
Aug. 3, 1844

In Memory of my
Beloved Father
Robert CURTIS
July 1, 1840
Jan. 28, 1923

Elizabeth G. CURTIS
Born Nov. 30, 1826
Died Nov. 8, 1884
Aged 68 yrs.
"Asleep in Jesus-Blessed
sleep
From which none never to
weep
Asleep in Jesus peaceful
rest
Whose waking is supremely
blest"

Ann E. CURTIS
Born August 24, 1851
Died August 26, 1855
She is not dead but sleepth
She has crossed
over the river

John L. CURTIS
Born
July 15, 1845
Died
March 12, 1905
He said while dying
Though I walk through the
valley and shadow of death
I will fear no evil.

T. C. CURTIS
Born Dec. 23, 1849
Died Feb. 7, 1874
Age 26

Ann G.
Wife of
W. C. CURTIS
Born
Nov. 20, 1859
Died
Mar. 8, 1886
Aged 26 years
3 months 16 days
insc. cannot read

Robert Grigs
CURTIS
Born Feb. 24, 1832
Died March 20, 1899

The following are transcribed by Gertrude Stead in 1994.

In Memory of
our Boy
Charley W. CURTIS
Born Dec. 8, 1892
Died June 22, 1910
Age 17 years 7 months 14 days
For he shall give his angels charge over thee to keep thee in all thy years

Charles CURTIS
Born
Nov. 10, 1866
Died
Oct 14, 1892
Age 25 yrs, 6 mo, 14 Days

Fannie S. CURTIS
Dec. 10, 1873
Feb. 9, 1939
God is Love
f/s (F.S.C.)

Hortense
CURTIS
Aug. 13, 1901
Oct. 4, 1907

Lizzie Gibb CURTIS
March 28, 1884
Feb. 1, 1948
She was a Christian woman

Mary E. CURTIS
Oct. 30, 1868
Jan. 23, 1933
At Rest

Lucie F. CURTIS
Wife of
Elder Robert
CURTIS
Born Dec. 7, 1816
Died July 8, 1915
Here Lies the Body

Murcer CURTIS
Mar. 22, 1887
Mar. 28, 1887

Miles C.
son of
John L. & V. C.
CURTIS
Born July 28, 1878
Died Oct. 8, 1895

Our Father, Elder
Robert C. CURTIS
1849 - 1919
The Book He Loved and Lived up to a Christian Rest

William Oliver
CURTIS
Feb. 23, 1859
July 10, 1935
Asleep in Jesus
f/s (W.O.C.)

Margaret E. JONES
Born
Oct. 23, 1876
Died
Aug. 30, 1894
Daughter of
Julia & Daniel O.
PATRICK, wife of
Dempsey D. JONES

Daniel C. PATRICK
Co. C.
32 Va. Inf
C.S.A.

Julia G. PATRICK
Wife of D. G. PATRICK
Born Nov. 13, 1845
Died Apr. 23, 1917
Age 71 years

Robt.Y. WEYMOUTH
Co. C.
Va. Inf.
SP. AM. WAR.

Margaret
CURTIS
Sept. 9, 1910
Oct. 12, 1911
Insc. cannot read.

John Y. CURTIS
Jan. 19, 1900
June 15, 1900

John E. CURTIS
Born
July 14, 1826
Died Aug. 1, 1882
Aged 22 yrs & 18 days
Insc. cannot read

*In memory of
my beloved Mother*
Mary E. CURTIS
Born March 26, 1844
Died Nov. 25, 1868

Pearlia CURTIS
Apr. 19, 1884
July 14, 1884

Our Darling
Ann C. GARROW
Born Nov. 11, 1883
Died April 16, 1886

In Memory of
Cornelia GARROW
Born
October 1885
Died
October 24, 1894

John GARROW
Born
June 30, 1846
Died
Feb. 25, 1860

Samuel GARROW
Born
Dec. 7, 180?
Died Nov. 12, 18?2
*Weep not Father and
Mother For me. For
I am Waiting in Glory for
Thee*

In Memory of
T. Gibbs
Son of
W. D. & Annie G.
CURTIS his wife
Born Sept. 15, 1885
Died July 6, 1886

Charles CURTIS
Born Nov. 10, 1866
Died Oct. 14, 1892
*Blessed are the Dead
which die in the Lord,
Hence Forth they rest from
their Labours and
Their Works Do Follow
Them.*

Anna E. CURTIS
Aug. 14, 1895
May 10, 1899

Daughter of
A. C. & H. V. CURTIS
Born
Dec. 16, 1901
Died
Aug. 4, 1902

No Name
Born
March 16, 1867
Died
Sept 12. 1881
*A Light from our
Home is Gone
A Voice once Loved is
Quiet*

Acknowledgment: Gertrude Stead for her research and photographs.

GARDEN OF EDEN
PENINSULA KOREAN BAPTIST CHURCH
GARROW GRAVEYARD

HARPERSVILLE ROAD (18) (36) {Q 30}

Myong Kum CHO
Deaconess
Jan. 14, 1900
Nov. 14, 1987

Kyu Young JUNG
Mar. 2, 1921
Jan. 18, 1988

David A. HOOVER
Sept. 29, 1962
Sept. 5, 1988

Christiana KIM
May 12, 1986
Aug. 11, 1994

Richard A. SENDER
SFC U. S. ARMY
1947 - 1987

Takeharu SAKAI
SGT MAJ US ARMY
Vietnam
Feb. 5, 1936
May 16, 1994

Kathleen Ilkyong PAENG
June 16, 1970
Sept. 26, 1986

Kenneth E. DUFFEY Jr.
MSGT US AIR FORCE
Vietnam   Persian Gulf
Jun. 12, 1950
May 11, 1994

Kwang Boon OH
Sept. 2, 1903
Jan 14, 1993

Yong Kap SO
1930 - 1992

So Sun KAP
October 5, 1919
October 30, 1992

Hyun Ja CHUN
Sept. 15, 1915
Nov. 22, 1993

This cemetery is an old cemetery the exact date is not known. The Garrow family was the original owner of the property. The Peninsula Korean Baptist Church was established near the site in 1974, and it is used by that church for burials.

There is one old grave from the original Garrow graveyard with a large stone with a Bronze plaque in the south corner of the Garden of Eden Cemetery, corner of Harpersville Road and Saunders Road.

The following information is from the *Virginia Historical Inventory, (W P A), The Library of Virginia.* Information was recorded in 1937.

In Memory of
D. P. JONES
Died Dec. 20, 1867
Aged 57

Acknowledgment: Gertrude Stead for researching records and transcribing markers.

D. P. Jones

Takeharu Sakai

DENBIGH BAPTIST CHURCH

MITCHELL POINT ROAD (5) {K 23}

The following is from 1937. *Virginia Historical Inventory, (W P A), Virginia State Library*.

The Episcopalians were the original owners of Denbigh Church. They owned it until about 1772. In 1744, the Baptists owned the church and are the present owners.

HISTORICAL SIGNIFICANCE;
A Baptist Church, known as "Denbigh", today occupies the site and exact position of an old church. The building which now stands has been rebuilt and added to, till there is no trace of the original structure.

Denbigh Church was formerly occupied by the Episcopal denomination. The first one was a Colonial church located a short distance from the present building. The earliest date could not be found, but it is known that there was a church there prior to 1744, because the second church was built in that year. We know this to be true because Bishop Meade writes in his history of "Old Churches' and Families of Virginia" that he visited Denbigh Church in 1854. It had been erected one hundred and ten years, and the weather boarding was still good. He states that the foundation of an older one was plainly to be traced a short distance in the woods which come up to the present church, which is only a few yards from the main Warwick Road, leading up and down the country.

Before or during the Revolutionary War, the Episcopal members became few in numbers, so the church was abandoned. It is said that they did this for the convenience of members who wished to go to the Bruton Church in Williamsburg or St. John's in Hampton. The last minister of Episcopal faith was the Reverend Mr. Camm, son of the Reverend Camm of Williamsburg. The glebe land was sold to Mr. Richard Young.

After the abandonment of the church by the Episcopalians, the building was used by several denominations. It is told that on the occasion of some very exciting meeting, when the old pews seemed to be in the way of promoting a revival, it was proposed from the pulpit that they be taken away, and benches put in place of them. This idea was about to be carried out, when a young man, whose ancestors had worshiped in the old church as it was, rose up and protested against it, saying that he would appeal to the law and prevent it.

This old church was first known by the name of "Tender branch". Later, it was called "Warwick Church". Sometime after 1810, "Denbigh Plantation" gave the church the glebe land which he had brought from the Episcopalians. The church still goes by the name of "Denbigh".

The first Baptist minister was Elder Matthews Wood. Dr. H. Pitts gives the following quotation, "He was native of Warwick County, he served the church until his death. He was a pious and useful preacher". Matthews Wood was a soldier in the First Virginia regiment. The transcription are also from the W P A records.

France W. TABB
Feb. 18, 1819
Died
Jan. 11, 1826

Edward TABB
July 30, 1814
Died
July 6, 1875

Here lies
Bennett Wood GREEN, MD.
Born April 6, 1835
In Warwick County, Virginia
Died July 31, 1873 at the
University of Virginia
Assistant Surgeon
U. S. Navy
Surgeon C.S.A. Navy

Mary E. JOHNSON
Born
May 18, 1842
Died
Dec. 26, 1898

In Memory of
Roberta I.
Wife of
Jessie WRIGHT
Born Feb. 8, 1939
Died Oct. 31, 1892

Sarah E.
Wife of
W. H. JURLINGTON

Born
Aug. 15, 1848
Died
Jan. 14, 1899

In Memory
of
Mary F. COPELAND, Nee JONES
Born March 11th 1829
Died March 4th 1915

John M. McINTOSH
Born Jan. 15, 1856
Died March 11, 1921

John W. LEWELLING
Jan. 3, 1847
Jan. 3, 1929
Gone but not forgotten

Armistead HAUGHTON
Born Sept. 7, 1839
Died April 13, 1916
Gone but not forgotten

Charles F. TILLOT
Born
March 25, 1837
Died
Sept. 19, 1917
Age 81 Yrs. 8 Mo. 25 Da.

William H. TILLOT
born
Aug. 16, 1838
Died
Sept. 29, 1908

Edward ALLEN
1842 - 1909

Father & Mother
John L. TABB
Born April 18, 1837
Died March 16, 1879

Fannie E. TABB
Born Sept. 10, 1836
Died Jan. 25, 1899

Sarah V. SCRIMINGER
Born
Nov. 9, 1855
Died
Oct. 12, 1898
A devoted wife
And a loving mother

J. E. SCRIMINGER
1857 - 1926

Rebecca HORNSBY
Mar. 14, 1854
Mar. 27, 1919
Death is of Eternal
Why would we weep

William HORNSBY
Feb. 22, 1844
Jan. 18, 1895

Allen James SYKES
Born
May 16, 1849
Died
May 27, 1911
At Rest

Annie R. JURLINGTON
Wife of
C. W. PARKER
Born Dec. 23, 1859
Died Dec. 2, 1912
An honest and faithful
mother

Denbigh Baptist Church Cemetery

Here Lyeth
The Body of Mary HARRISON
Daughter of the Honorable Cole DIGGES, Esq.
President of his Magtrs Council of the Colony
and
Late wife of Colonel Nathaniel HARRISON
of Prince George County
By whom she had four children viz
Nathaniel who was born May 27, 1740
Diggs who was born Oct. 22 and
died Nov. 12, 1740
(both interred near this place)
Also Elizabeth born July 30th 1737
Benjamin born Feb. 13, 1742
She so discharged the several duties
of a Wife, Mother, Daughter, Neighbor
that her Relations and Acquaintances Might justly
estimate their affections
Was it not chastened with the unsupported Remembrance
that every virtue which adds weight to the loss Augments her reward
Obit Nov. 12, 1774   Oct 27

Front Section of the Church, transcribed by Mr. Hutchinson's Boy Scouts Troop # 108.

Floyd R. WOODFIN
Sept. 6, 1870
Feb. 13, 1934

Sarah H. WOODFIN
Jan. 7, 1884
June 23, 1961

Cora Lee ROWE
Dec. 25, 1871
Aug. 29, 1957

William C. ROWE
Florida
Seaman U.S. Navy
November 25, 1931
Age 73

Powell W. MASON
PFC US Army
World War II
Aug. 14, 1920
Jan. 16, 1993

Flora Belle
MASON
1898 - 1961

Thomas Henry
MASON
1898 - 1961

Eugene Jackson
GARRETT
September 7, 1866
April 4, 1947

Elvira Cavileer
GARRETT
November 10, 1874
February 21, 1944

Ida Estelle
GARRETT
December 15, 1911
November 27, 1949

Joseph Daniel
PARKER
1888 - 1936

Irma Topping
PARKER
1895 - 1934

Samuel F. DOLAN
Nov. 7, 1891
Mar. 18, 1982
d/s w/Margaret D.

Margaret D. DOLAN
Feb. 10, 1896
Aug. 10, 1949

Violet Parker MASON
August 17, 1916
April 24, 1940

Edward J. MAGILLEY
Aug. 8, 1863
Dec. 1, 1931

George W. KELLUM
Dec. 18, 1859
Jan. 5, 1928
His wife
Emma D. KELLUM
Nov. 19, 1863
June 11, 1931
f/s E.D.K.
f/s G.W.K.

Wm. J. BONEWELL
Born Nov. 7, 181?
Died Mar. (?)8, 1872
(only portions of the
inscriptions can be read}

In memory of
Mrs. Ann BONEWELL
Born March 13, 1805
Died March 1, 1869
Dear are ____ to the grave
Though lonely it's repose
and thou shall arise
and bloom like Sharon's
Rose

Annie Bell PARKER
Aug. 3, 1881
June 4, 1887

John Revel PARKER
March 14, 1844
Oct. 10, 1901

Jane SCRIMINGER
Oct. 20, 1859
May 15, 1919

John Edward PARKER
June 4, 1885
Sept. 19, 1970

Sarah Jane Fox PARKER
Sept. 13, 1891
March 28, 1977

John Edward PARKER, Jr.
Jan. 6, 1921
Aug. 19, 1921

Henry LINWOOD
W. S. & S. O. READ
Born
Sept. 13, 1909
Died
July 26, 1925

Infant Daughter
of Mr. & Mrs.
R. T. HOSTETTER
Aug. 1, 1929

Father
Charles MELZER
1845 - 1921

Mother
Anna MELZER
1857 - 1946

At Rest
Sarah E. HALL
Sept. 29, 1846
Nov. 2, 1920
*In Memory of my
grandmother*

Annie Virginia
HALL
Jan. 2, 1892
July 12, 1892
Safe in the arms ?
f/s A.V.H.

Husband
William B.
HALL
Oct. 26, 1865
Dec. 19, 1920
*There are no partings
in heaven*

William C. BURNHAM
1856 - 1946
Clerk of Warwick County
from July 1, 1899
to Dec. 31, 1919

Jesse KELLUM
Born Feb. 26, 1819
Died
Nov. 26, 1884
Aged 65 Years
*Mark the Perfect Man
and behold the upright
for the end of Greatness is
peace*
f/s J.K.

Erected by William *and
Mary
to the memory of their
beloved mother*
Elizabeth KELLUM
Born Nov. 15, 1829
Died June 29, 1896
*Without a thought
of pain or death
And yet at times my eyes
are wet with tears for
he I cannot see
Oh Mother art thou living
yet and dost thou still
remember me*

Margie McINTOSH
Born
July 4, 1845
Died
Oct. 25, 1898
*Dearest sister thou hast
left us
Here thy lost we deeply
feel
But tis God who hast bereft
us
He can all our sorrows
heal*

Marcacel
wife of J. KELLUM
Married 1840
Died Oct. 22, 1869
Aged 45 years
f/s M. K.

Margaret S. PARKER
Born Jun. 27, 1831
Died Oct. 2, 1876
*Sister thou whose mild and
lovely
Gentle as the summer
breeze
Pleasant as the air of
evening
When it floats among the
trees*

In memory of
Edward T. PARKER
Born Mar. 14, 1844
Died April 10, 1874
Age 30 years of 27 days

BURCHER
(Marker)

Here Lyeth
the Body of Mary HARRISON
Daughter of the Hon. Cole DIGGES, Esq.
President of this Maj. Council for this Colony
and
Late wife of Colonel Nathaniel HARRISON
of Prince George County
By whom she had four children viz.
Nathaniel who was born May 27, 1739
and died June 25, 1740
Digges who was born October 22 & died Nov. 12, (?)
(both interred near this place)
also Elizabeth born July 30th 1737
Benjamin born February ?, 1742
She so discharged the several duties
of a Wife, Mother, Daughter, Neighbour
that her Relatives & Acquaintance
might justly esteem their affection is supportable
Was it not cliaftifed with the Remembrance
That every Virtue which adds weight to their lots
Augments her reward
Obiit Xov. 12, 1711 At 27

Scared to the memory of my dear husband
Sammuel Y. McINTOSH
Born Oct 4, 1837
Died Dec. 20, 1897
Are you prepared
to meet your god?
The Lord is my Shephard
I shall (rest chipped off)

My Dear Wife
Maggie
SHACKELFORD
Dec. 18, 1870
Nov. 26, 1938
At Rest

Wemmie Rowe MORGAN
April 10, 1860
August 2, 1891

Father
J. W. MORGAN
Oct. 14, 1851
Jan. 21, 1900

Father
Franklin
SEBURN
May 5, 1867
Dec. 14, 1929
*Weep not, he is at
Rest*

Rebecca
HORNSBY
Mar. 10, 1854
Mar. 27, 1919
d/s w/ William

William
HORNSBY
Feb. 22, 1844
Jan. 19, 1895
d/s w/ Rebecca
Inscription for both
*Death is eternal life, why
should we weep*

Romelus
HORNSBY
Sept. 15, 1859
Feb. 9, 1926
d/s w/ Alice S.

Alice S.
HORNSBY
July 3, 1873
July 11, 1925
d/s w/ Romelus

Robert L. TURLINGTON
1872 - 1898

Grace F. TURLINGTON
1895 - 1895

*In memory of
our beloved Father*
B. F. TURLINGTON
Died June 28, 1891
Age 39 yrs.
*Dearest father, thou hast left us
Here thy loss we deeply feel.
Bit tis God who hath bereft us
He can all our sorrows heal.*

Mother
Georgie Turlington
PHAUP
Dec. 24, 1867
Dec. 13, 1933

Mother
Susie Smith
EVERSICH
June 7, 1882
June 5, 1938

In God We Trust
Andrew J. TURLINGTON
Born
Nov. 1, 1869
Died
Jan. 13, 1897

Sarah F.
wife of
W. H. TURLINGTON
Born
Aug. 15, 1848
Died
Jan. 11, 1899
At Rest

Bettie E. OWENS
1860 - 1922
d/s w/ William

William A. OWENS
1852 - 1919
d/s w/ Bettie E.

Father
Benjamin F. PETERS
Born
Apr. 12, 1836
Died
March 4, 1862
Gone but not forgotten
d/s w/ Mary E.
f/s B.F.P.

Mother
Mary E.
Wife of
Benjamin F. PETERS
Born Feb. 28, 1842
Died May 27, 1925
Asleep in Jesus
f/s M.E.P.

Edmond F. PETERS
April 26, 1861
Oct. 10, 1870
f/s E.F.P.

Matthew PETERS
1849 - 1871

In memory of
Roberta L.
wife of
Jessie WRIGHT
Born Feb. 8, 1829
Died Oct. 31, 1892
Aged 53 yrs. 9 mos. 23 dys
Now if we be dead with Christ
We believe that we shall also live with him

Jessie WRIGHT
Sept. 28, 1848
July 27, 1899
At Rest

William S. HAWLEY
1860 - 1948
d/s w/ Sallie A.
f/s W.S.H.

Sallie A. HAWLEY
1867 - 1958

Paul E. HAWLEY
Dec. 1, 1904
July 27, 1904
f/s P.E.H.

Cpl.
James H. T. HAWLEY
CO H.
32 VA INF
CSA

Laura B.
wife of
Wm. S. HAWLEY
Born Nov. 5, 1876
Dies Aug. 8, 1888
Inscription unreadable

TAYLOR Children

Mother
Annie E.
1864 - 1947

Father
John H. TAYLOR
1857 - 1915

Son
John D. TAYLOR
1893 - 1915

Cousin
Frank WATSON
1886 - 1916

TAYLOR
Son
W. Howard
1903 - 1963

Wilton George HOGGE
US Navy
World War II
June 24, 1924
Aug 9, 1974

Willie T. TURLINGTON
1898 - 1899

John William MORGAN
July 15, 1883
July 2, 1944

Sarah Walters MORGAN
Nov. 22, 1897
June 24, 1934

Lottie H. PETERS
Aug 26, 1885
Nov. 15, 1934

William G. PETERS
Jan. 22, 1865
Nov. 13, 1934

Elizabeth A. SMITH
April 9, 1844
Dec. 23, 1907

William H. MALLICOTTE
1871 - 1954

John E. MALLICOTTE
1876 - 1915

George I. MALLICOTTE
1907 - 1908

James D. MALLICOTTE
1905 - 1905

Pauline MALLICOTTE
1899 - 1899

Reginald MORGAN
March 12, 1905
July 3, 1906

Daisy Moore MORGAN
Nov. 20, 1882
Nov. 17, 1914

Bettie Lee LEWIS
June 24, 1929
July 7, 1945

Baby (Unknown)

The following is from the rear section behind the church.

Mark S. DeBERRY
Oct. 11, 1893
Mar. 18, 1950

Jeanette K.
DeBERRY
Mar. 22, 1896
Jan. 11, 1985

Mark Wayne DeBERRY
Nov. 4, 1942
April 15, 1943
Safe in the arms of Jesus
f/s M.W.D.

Lorraine F. DeBERRY
Oct. 11, 1922
d/s w/ Lenmere L.

Lenmere L. DeBERRY Sr
July 26, 1915
Dec 13, 1988
d/s w/ Lorraine F.

Mary MADISON
1891 - 1979
d/s w/ W. B.

W. B. MADISON
1887 - 1942
d/s w/ Mary
f/s W.B.

Eli N. Cke (?)
illegible

Mary Letha
MUNSON
1877 - 1930

Annie E.
HARRIS
Sept. 15, 1893
June 15, 1896

Willie A.
HARRIS
Nov. 21, 1900
May 27, 1902

Mildred H.
HARRIS
Dec. 18, 1909
Dec. 18, 1909

Richard T. HARRIS
Feb. 8, 1867
March 17, 1947
d/s w/ Martha I.

Martha I. HARRIS
Nov. 9, 1872
Jan. 15, 1951

Earl H. BOZARD
December 1, 1900
September 12, 1987

Edward T. OWENS
March 2, 1885
Oct. 9, 1946
d/s w/ Lille O.

Lille O. BOZARD
April 16, 1896
May 11, 1986
d/s w/ Edward T.

HARRIS

Catharine HARRIS
1847 - 1914

Jennette
Born Sept. 26, 1906
Died Aug. 13, 1907
Infant Dan
Born Nov. 25, 1897
Died Nov. 25, 1897
Children of
R. M. & Annie O.
HARRIS
At Rest

Laura Fox PALACK
1846 - 1931

Joseph J. PALACK
1902 - 1938

Husband
Samuel G.
SMITH
Born
Aug. 15, 1888
Died
Aug. 15, 1912
*Dearest husband
thou hast left us And
thy loss we deeply feel
This the Lord that has
bereft us of one we
loved so well*
SMITH

Mother
Viola Sreves
FOX
Dec. 7, 1892
Feb. 15, 1981
wife of
Benjamin C. FOX
REST IN PEACE

Mother
Anna E. FOX

Aldicut W. SREVES
Aug. 6, 1867
Dec. 17, 1834
*Blessed are the pure in heart
for they shall see God*

Etta F.
Daughter of
G. L. FOX
Aug. 27, 1894
Sept. 20, 1894
Gone to be an angel

Sarah Frances FOX
1870 - 1906
d/s w/ George L.

George Leroy FOX
1865 - 1947
d/s w/ Sarah F.

PALLACK
footstone

Delbert C. FOX
Dec. 17, 1917
Dec. 21, 1917

Francis W. TABB
Feb. 18, 1819
Died
Jan. 11, 1896
d/s w/ Edward

Edward TABB
July 24, 1814
Died
July 6, 1873
d/s w/ Francis W.
*So he bringeth them
into their desired haven
ps. 107.30vs.*

Sarah Lucas
TABB
Died Nov. 22, 1910
Aged 60 years
*Whosoever Liveth
And Believeth in Me
Shall never Die*

Burleigh Harrison
WALKER
Feb 9, 1870
Sept. 26, 1956
d/s w/ Ruth C.

Ruth Campbell
WALKER
Jan. 18, 1887
May 20, 1920
d/s w/ Burleigh

Annie R.
TURLINGTON
Wife of
C. W. PARKER
Born Dec. 23, 1859
Died Dec. 2, 1912
*An honest and faithful
mother
Gone but not forgotten
Mother*
f/s APR.

Our Brother
Russell Clayton
WALKER
Born
April 3, 1872
Died
June 10, 1898
Asleep in Jesus Blessed Sleep
f/s RCW

Ellen James SYKES
Born
May 16, 1849
Died May 29, 1911
At Rest
f/s E.J.S.

Maggie Parker
WHISPELL
Nov. 15, 1876
Oct. 17, 1918
Asleep In Jesus

W. Lacy FOWLER
Born Nov. 17, 1899
Died Oct. 4, 1907
*Gone but not
forgotten
Mother*
f/s WLF

Mary E. JOHNSON
Born
May 18, 1842
Died
Dec. 26, 1898
*She's left this world of woe
For regions of eternal love
T'was God who
called her from below
to join in praising him above*
f/s MEJ

Jacob H. JOHNSON
Died Nov. 2, 1895
Aged 37 yrs
2 mos. 9 days
Gone but not forgotten
f/s JHJ

FOWLER
f/s
Sallie F. FOWLER
Oct. 13, 1868
July 10, 1932
w/ William J.

f/s
William J. FOWLER
Oct. 4, 1862
April 14, 1950

Here lies
Bennett Wood GREEN M. D.
Born April 6, 1835
In Warwick County Va
Died July 31, 1913 At the
*University of Virginia
Assistant Surgeon
US Navy
Surgeon CSA Navy
An Alumnus
And benefactor of the
University of Virginia*

John Alden YOUNG M.D.
Born
in Warwick County
June 28, 1854
Died Apr. 3, 1918
*A County Doctor who
gave his life to the poor*

Martha Anne MASON
July 25, 1893
d/s w/ John Oley

John Oley MASON
Nov. 9, 1889
March 21, 1970
d/s w/ Martha Anne

Marylou B. GILMAN
1905 - 1964
Jesus said "I am the resurrection and the life."

Grave Unknown

Ben H. WILLIAMS Sr.
Virginia
Pvt. Co C 717 Ry
OPR BN TC
World War II
Oct. 21, 1926
March 5, 1969

Ernest PHAUP
April 22, 1923
April 19, 1938
At Rest

John L. PARKER Sr.
Oct. 3, 1884
June 30, 1966

Eather O. PARKER
*In Loving Memory -
Children*
Feb. 3, 1890
Aug. 21, 1974

Perry W. ELROD Jr.
Virginia
S. Sgt U. S. Army
Korea Vietnam
Aug. 30, 1927
July 18, 1973

Thomas E. PHAUP
May 28, 1900
July 16, 1956

Mary H. PHAUP
July 30, 1904
Oct. 30, 1977

Father
Thomas F. ROWE
Born July 29, 1851
Died Jan. 16, 1946

Mother
Emeline Elizabeth
Wife of
Thomas F. ROWE
Born Mar. 25, 1859
Died Dec. 14, 1924
As a wife devoted
As a mother affectionate
As a Friend kind and true
f/s E.E.R.

Vernon Elmore DAVIS
May 9, 1890
Nov. 11, 1976

Senie Moss DAVIS
May 19, 1899
Sept. 18, 1976

John L. DAVIS
Dec 23, 1872
Apr. 22, 1940
d/s w/ Blanche

Blanche DAVIS
Feb. 25, 1899
Oct. 15, 1965
d/s w/ John L.

Our Daughter
Lauren Davis HUNT
1897 - 1924

Gladys Pearl
WRIGHT
Apr. 8, 1912
Nov. 15, 1915
Now with the angels

Robert Emil ALTWEGG
Born Sept. 19, 1893
In Sulgen, Switzerland
Died Aug. 31, 1971

Genevieve Bonewell
ALTWEGG
Born Aug. 27, 1903
in Morrison, Virginia
Died July 7, 1988

Wilson M. LYNCH
Jan 14, 1869
Oct. 6, 1934
d/s w/ Fannie B.

Fannie B. LYNCH
May 29, 1897
Feb. 13, 1961
Wife   Husband
d/s w/ Wilson M.

Grave Unknown

Ethel B. DAVIS
Aug. 20, 1900
Sept. 24, 1903
Gone to be an angel
f/s EBD

Alice A. DAVIS
Dec. 26, 1870
Nov. 22, 1938
d/s w/ James G.

James G. DAVIS
Sept. 30, 1865
May 6, 1936
d/s w/ Alice A.

William H.
DAVIS
Dec. 4, 1870
Apr. 29, 1924
Asleep in Jesus

N. M. GODSEY
Feb. 6, 1873
Feb. 2, 1920

Grady R.
BONEWELL
1891 - 1918

BONEWELL
James F. BONEWELL
1861 - 1921
Sarah E. BONEWELL
1867 - 1952
Mother Father

TABB
f/s
John E. TABB
1875 - 1940

Sarah Elizabeth
HOWARD
May 12, 1858
Jan. 15, 1935
At Rest
f/s SEH

Charles
BONEWELL
1866 - 1911
f/s CB

Edward ALLEN
1842 - 1909
f/s EA

Father and Mother
John L. TABB
Born April 13, 1837
Died March 15, 1879

Fannie E. TABB
Born Sept. 10, 1836
Died Jan. 25, 1899
Jesus said: I am the resurrection and the life
He that believeth on me though he were
dead,
yet shall he live.

John B. CHILDRESS
Nov. 20, 1872
Aug. 2, 1913
f/s JBC
d/s w/ Lelia A.

Lelia A. CHILDRESS
Mar. 16, 1866
Apr. 25, 1960
f/s LAC
d/s w/ John B.

Britt ROLVIX

Mary F. HOPKINS
Born
Oct. 11, 1837
Died
May 5, 1918
Told her, O father is thine arms and let her
henceforth be
a messenger of love between
Our Human hearts and thee.

Norris H. PAXSON Jr.
1906 - 1980

Carolyn S. PAXSON
1911 - 1987

SCRIMINGER
(no other readable Markings)

Rosa Etta
wife of
William S. McINTOSH
March 13, 1862
Aug. 16, 1900
She has gone to the
mansions of rest
f/s R.E.McI

A. L. McINTOSH
Born
May 12, 1882
Died
Oct. 30, 1899
Although he sleeps
his memory dith live
And cheering comforts
to his mourners give
He followed virtue
as his truest guide
Lived as a Christian
as a Christian died
f/s ALM

H. C. SCRIMINGER
1831 - 1913

Hettie SCRIMINGER
Born Nov. 10, 1838
Died Feb. 3, 1897
One precious to
our hearts has gone
The voice that we loved is stilled
The place made vacant in our house
Can never more be filled
Our
Father in his wisdom called
The Boon his love had given
And though on earth the body lie
The soul is safe in heaven
f/s H. S.

Our Baby
Robert H.
Son of
H G & M H
HOLLOWAY
July 29, 1926
Our loved one

Our Baby
Infant Daughter of
H G & M H
HOLLOWAY
Aug. 8, 1929
Our loved one

Helen M. HOLLOWAY
1902 - 1962
f/s H.M.H.

Cora H. SCRIMINGER
1878 - 1941
f/s C.H.S.

J. H. SCRIMINGER
1857 - 1926
f/s J.H.S.

Sarah V. SCRIMINGER
Born
Nov. 9, 1855
Died
Oct. 12, 1898
*A beloved wife
and a loving mother*
f/s S.V.S.

Julius L. SCRIMINGER
Nov. 20, 1888
Dec. 11, 1943
f/s J.L.S.

Ada G. WELLS
1884 - 1976
f/s A.G.W.

Virginia B. BURCHER
March 19, 1894
Aug. 7, 1961

Clifton C. BURCHER
April 13, Sept 24
1889   1959

Lila M. GARRETT
1915 - 1952

Carl E.
Son of C. C. and Nina R.
BURCHER
Born Aug. 2, 1918
Died May 6, 1981

William H. TILLOT
Born
Aug. 16, 1838
Died
Sept. 29, 1908

Charles T. TILLOT
Born
March 25, 1837
Died
Sept. 19, 1917
Aged 81 yrs, 5 mos,
25 days
Gone but not forgotten

Acie A. OWENS
July 29, 1883
June 7, 1955

Hattie B. OWENS
Sept. 1, 1889
June 7, 1956

William Armistead
HAUGHTON
Jan. 7,   May 23,
1908   1989

Philip Roscoe
son of
P E & K L COOKE
Born Apr. 24, 1916
Died Oct. 22, 1918
The angels called him

Lula Vernella
Daughter of
P E & K L COOKE
Born Dec. 8, 1910
Died Jan. 26, 1913
*A little bud of love
To bloom with God above*
f/s L.V.C.

Mark A. LAND
Aug. 8, 1958
Jan. 25, 1977

Our Darling
Woodrow Wilson
HAUGHTON
Born May 18, 1913
Died Aug. 1, 1913
Baby

Mother
Annie C. HAUGHTON
Jan. 20,   Feb. 12,
1886   1973
*The Lord is my shepherd,
I shall not want*

Father
R. E. HAUGHTON
Born
June 7, 1886
Died
July 30, 1945
Our Loved One

Father
Benjamin C. FOX
Oct. 8, 1888
June 25, 1965

Son
Milton F. FOX
Feb. 13, 1913
April 2, 1961

Albert W. SREVES
May 15, 1864
March 11, 1959

Charlie C. FOX
Aug. 1, 1884
Nov. 6, 1955
f/s
w/ Olive Fox

Olive Fox HAYES
May 26, 1900
Aug. 26, 1983
f/s
w/ Charlie C.

Thomas Joseph
HOGGE
Dec. 12, 1872
Feb. 4, 1916
Father
d/s w/ Irene Lee

Irene Lee
HOGGE
Oct. 1, 1879
May 30, 1968
Mother
d/s w/ Thomas J.

f/s
Frank Lee CURTIS
1898 - 1952

Elizabeth HOUGHTON
Mar. 10, 1930
Mar. 11, 1930
f/s EH

J. Langhorne
HOUGHTON
Aug. 23, 1900
May 5, 1941
f/s JLH

Elizabeth Black
HOUGHTON
June 15, 1904
Oct 4, 1941
f/s EBH

HOUGHTON
Robert   Alda S.
1870 - 1952   1867 - 1944

Thelma G.
FOX-CORBITT
March 31, 1917
Jan. 20, 1969

Sarah M. LLEWELLYN
1879 - 1933

Ruby O. LLEWELLYN
1907 - 1933

John A. LLEWELLYN
1874 - 1965

Fern Llewellyn
CHANDLER
1918 - 1987

Unmarked Grave

Unmarked Grave

Unmarked Grave

Unmarked Grave

Unmarked Grave

Earl Arthur PARKER
Virginia
SF3 USNR
World War II
July 14, 1921
Aug. 21, 1957

Husband
Victor F. PARKER
1908 - 1951

Edward J. VAIL
1890 - 1962

M. C. OWENS Jr.
Son of
M. C. and Bessie
OWENS
Born Nov. 7, 1905
Died April 10, 1910
Gone but not forgotten

Willie M. HOGGE
1910 - 1981

HOGGE
William Everette HOGGE
Oct 15, 1887-
May 25, 1934
His wife
Norrie Lee HOGGE
Aug. 13, 1891
Sept 23, 1938
f/s
O my darling how I miss you
No one Knows the tears I shed
but in heaven I hope to meet you
Where no farewell words are said
His wife

ENOS
William Warner   Mildred Hogge
Oct 27 1915   Jan 1 1916
May 12 1984

HOGGE
Daisy   Thomas Franklin Jr
May 31, 1923   Jan 1, 1925
Apr 23, 1937   June 6, 1947

Grace TRUMAN   Thomas FRANKLIN Sr
Sept 20 1897   Apr 8 1893
July 18 1980   Oct 5 1949

David Mercer GRIFFIN
1892 - 1939

James Mercer ALLRED
1943 - 1946

Anthony GEORGE
Born 1904
Died April 25 1930
*To know him was
to love him*

Elizabeth Parker DONNELLY
April 19 1883
April 4 1959

Walter Lee
Son of
F J and E B BISHOP
Nov 3 1922
May 16 1923

Paul A. WHITE
June 27 1900
June 8 1987

Wife
Lola P. WHITE
Oct 6 1902
May 12 1974

Father
Pelham A. WHITE
Nov 4 1874
Mar 19 1927

Mother Lucy Ray WHITE
Aug 11, 1867
July 6, 1935

Brother
Robert E. WHITE
Dec. 20, 1903
June 2, 1962

BLACK
Wm. J. BLACK
Aug. 23, 1879
Mar. 20, 1942
foot stone

William T. BLACK
Born June 24, 1851
Died May 25, 1924

PARKER
Thomas H.   Edward L.
1878 - 1965   1878 - 1959

Cora Lukhard HOPKINS
February 10, 1879
October 22, 1941
*Resting in hope of a
Glorious Resurrection*

Major L.
Son of
W H & M J
----- (Crack)
Mar. 9, 1914
Feb. 1, 1922
Asleep in Jesus

John M. McINTOSH
Born July 10, 1857
Died June 14, 1945

CURTIS
Mother	Father
Georgie Haughton	Arthur Curtis
March 31 1865	May 24 1859
Nov 13 1926	Jan 5 1942

PATRICK
Fitzhugh	Elizabeth
February 11, 1897	February 14, 1843
March 24, 1940	July 16, 1946

Freddie PATRICK
Sept 20 1893
March 8 1963

John W. WALTERS
Sept 30 1887
Sept 4 1960
foot stone

Martha L. WALTERS
April 24 1875
April 7 1965
foot stone

WALTERS
John J.	Martha Jane
July 17 1849	Jun 1 1880
Jan 28 1922	Aug 18 1955

Armistead HAUGHTON
Born Sept. 7, 1839
Died April 13, 1916
Gone but not forgotten

Charlotte W.
HAUGHTON
Wife of
John W.
LEWELLING
Born July 10, 1843
Died Feb. 28, 1914
Gone but not forgotten

John W.
LEWELLING
Jan. 3, 1847
Jan. 3, 1929

In Memory of
Edward H. DAVIS
Born Feb 14, 1895
Died May 15, 1920
*Asleep in Jesus Blessed Sleep
in which none ever wake to weep*

HARRIS
Robert M. HARRIS
Oct. 6, 1872 July 23, 1934
His wife
Annie O. HARRIS
May 26, 1869 July 23, 1934
Gone but not forgotten

Mother
Audrey V.
HEYWOOD
May 31, 1922
Oct. 13, 1986

Carrie Jones
NORTHROP
Oct. 12, 1892
May 20, 1943

Magruder B.
JONES
Sept. 20, 1861
Dec. 28, 1934

Cora B.
JONES
Dec. 31, 1869
Jan. 13, 1952

Helen J.
JOHNSON
Aug. 16, 1896
Nov. 25, 1979

Frank E.
JOHNSON
Nov. 29, 1926
Aug. 27, 1985

Thomas W. WALTERS
1891 - 1940

Gloria A. WALTERS
1927 - 1929

Nettie M. WALTERS
1897 - 1971

MALLICOTT
John M.
1873 - 1942

Mother
Margaret E.
MALLICOTT
Oct. 4, 1880

Wm. Morris HEYWOOD
son of
Mr. & Mrs. W. T. HEYWOOD
born Aug 11, 1917
died May 22, 1934
Living with Jesus

Walter Thomas HEYWOOD
Dec. 10, 1878 - May 27, 1936

Catherine I. Heywood MILLS
July 26, 1896 - Dec. 10, 1961

Father
Homer L. F.
HEYWOOD
July 10, 1919
Sept. 9, 1960

William Y. JONES
Jan. 14, 1853
Aug. 8, 1935

In memory of
Mary F. COPELAND nee JONES
born March 11th, 1829
died March 4th, 1915

Linnie R. MASON
Feb. 21, 1891
July 17, 1940

Joan Ann
infant
daughter of
R. H. & M. A. GIBSON
Nov. 27, 1940
Mar. 16, 1941

GAMBOL GRAVEYARD

MARINER MUSEUM, NOLAN TRAIL (21) {H 33}

Today there are no tombstones. They have been destroyed through the years. The following is a history, from *"The History and Development of Mariners' Museum Park: 1929 - 1936*. By Dr. Harold Cones, Christopher Newport University, Newport News, Va.

BRIEF HISTORY:

"The deed to the property of which W. Taylor Ham was executor contained an obligation to protect the family cemetery. Located on the Ham property was an historical house referred to as the *"Copeland House"*, built sometime around 1745. The only documents bearing on the history of the House were in the will of John Gambol, which is dated 1848, and in the original deed to the House when purchased by John Gambol, about 1823. Gambol also owned the old mill and the mill house on the Museum property. The mill house being known at the time of Museum purchase as the Harlow House, from the name of its most recent tenant. The mill and mill house were sold by Gambol to the Causeys, who in turn sold to the Old Dominion Land Corporation. After Gambol's death in 1852, his property passed to his two married daughters, Anna Ham and Henrietta Copeland, from whom the house took its name. When The Mariners' Museum purchased the property, a clause was placed in the property transfer document which stated:

> Entry of heirs and descendants of John Gambol, deceased, their servants and agents to visit the Gambol family burying ground and provide for the care, upkeep and maintenance of all of the graves therein along ways to be provided by A. M. Huntington so long as they remain. Also, within twelve months from March 19, 1930 permit disinterment and removal of all bodies now interred therein upon condition that the graves will be filled and level to protect the burying ground from erosion caused by the rising of the water by artificial means so long as the burying ground is preserved and maintained by the descendants of John Gambol.

The Museum offered the heirs the opportunity to disinter the bodies but they declined. Several months after the purchase, the Museum built a protective low brick wall around the burying ground, which was located on a point of land at the very edge of the lake."

The following is from the Virginia Historical Inventory, (W P A), The Library of Virginia.

1937.
There are five tombstones in this little family burying ground. The Mariners' Museum has built a brick wall about four feet high around the graves for protection. The graveyard is situated on the point of a ridge on the east bank of the creek and is overgrown with underbrush.

Tombstone transcribed by (W P A)

John GAMBOL
Born Feby. 2, 1802
Died Oct. 20, 1852
Blessed are the Dead
Which die in the Lord

Mrs Mary Ann CURTIS
Feb. 1818
Died Oct. 29, 1855

Jno. THOMPSON
Co. H.
36th
N. Y. Inf.

Mary A. C. COPELAND
1855 - 1877

Martha J. GAMBOL
Born March 8, 1851
Died August 30, 1855

James T. GAMBOL
1846 - 1869

Mary E. GAMBOL
1842 - 1862

William GAMBOL

There are no tombstones on this site today (1997).

Acknowledgment: Gertrude Stead for research and photographs.

The Gambol Graveyard as it looked in 1997

GARROW CEMETERY
NEWPORT NEWS CITY PARK (49) {p 10}

From the *Denbigh Gazette*, February 23, 1994.
"On April 3, 1862, McClellan had his advance stopped and dug in. Smith's division was on the shores of the Warwick River in what is present day Newport News City Park. The 3rd and 4th Vermont were dug in on Garrow's farm with the 5th and 6th close at hand.

Ann Garrow (nee Curtis), a widow, had lost her husband, Private J. T. Garrow, when he became sick while serving with the Warwick Beauregards who were encamped just up river at Wynne's Mill. Private Garrow died at home and his remains now rest in a cemetery just off Susan Constant Drive in upper Denbigh.

The Garrow house stood just about where Newport News City Park's interpretive center now stands. In fact, directly behind the center, brick rubble from the Garrow house's chimneys are still visible.

With Ann Garrow was her son James Toomer Garrow and Daughter Ann. Their farm had been named "Merry Oaks" by her late husband, John. However, in April of 1862, it would be far from merry." There is more in this article on what was happening during the Civil War.

From the Denbigh Gazette, March 1994. "On the morning of April 18th a Confederate officer came to mid-point on the dam (now in Newport News City Park) under a flag of truce. Here he met with a Vermont officer and arranged for the 29 Vermonters who were killed on the Confederate side to be returned to the Union side.

An appropriate site on the Garrow farm was selected for a cemetery. Ranger Jerry Bochek's research comes into play here. As the graves were being dug, remains of Revolutionary War soldiers were uncovered. Bochek's research indicates that they were British troops as the distinctive breast plates that British Infantry men wore were in with the remains of those soldiers from some 90 years before. The actual attacks resulted in the Vermonters having 44 men killed and 148 wounded. However, of the 148 wounded Green Mountain Boys, 21 of them would die from wounds sustained during the two attacks. No actual count of Confederate casualties were listed, as they were included in the toll of casualties during the battle of Williamsburg fought in early May. Supposition is that Confederates lost over 20 killed in action and around 50 were wounded, primarily of the 15th North Carolina. Absolutely nothing was accomplished or gained with the battle. On the night of May 1, 1862 the Confederates abandoned the Warwick River Line and retreated back to a defensive position outside of Williamsburg.

On the morning of May 2, 1862 the Union forces walked across the dam without a shot being fired. Several Union officers took note of the fortifications and were astounded. The positions were three and four positions deep a definite challenge which would have produced an extreme amount of Union casualties had the attack been re-initiated.

The fallen Vermonters laid to rest on the Garrow Farm were moved in 1866 to the National Military Cemetery in Yorktown. Here, to this day, the Green Mountain Boys lay in rest, including the (Sleeping Sentry William Scott)."
The graves have been removed to the Yorktown National Cemetery.
Acknowledgment: Gertrude Stead for her research.

HARWOOD CEMETERY

ENDVIEW PLANTATION (16) {O 3}

Harwood Family Cemetery Endview

The Harwood Garden Cemetery

The following transcriptions are from, *Virginia Historical Inventory (W P A), The Library of Virginia.*

Mother
L. M. T. HARWOOD
b. Jan. 1835
d. Dec. 1864

Father
H. K. HARWOOD
b. Sept. 1830
d. 1901

E. M. HARWOOD
b. Dec. 1855
d. Aug. 1876

D. G. H. HARWOOD
b. Feb. 1860
d. Dec 1870

N. L. HARWOOD
b. Jan. 1859
d. Sept. 1864

In Memory of
John L. HARWOOD
Born in Warwick
Co. Va. June 7, 1836
Died in Norfolk, Va.
Jan. 30, 1890

"There appears to be a very worn sandstone marker located here also. The general area is covered with periwinkle, there could be additional graves, but the markers are gone.

The graves are located as follows; Facing the front of the house, proceed to the southeast rear corner of the house, continue in a southeasterly direction through the field, cross the creek bed and continue up the wooded hill on the other side to an open field. The cemetery is in the general area of the north side. The site of the circa 1720, Harwood house is located across the next field past the cemetery in the same southeasterly direction."

There are two gravestones in the garden to the west of the house, one is not legible today. The other is partially legible.

> ----- CURTIS
> b. Feb. 25, 1898
> d. June 29, 1899
> Daughter of ---- CURTIS
> and R. T. CURTIS"

There is much history to Endview Plantation. The following is from the *Denbigh Gazette June 5, 1996.*

"The Endview Plantation house is the oldest in Newport News. In the near future it will be restored and turned into a tourist attraction featuring a major museum and a Civil War Campus with living history sites on 300 acres that begin near the corner of Jefferson Avenue and Yorktown Road.

The Endview Plantation house was built sometime prior to 1720 by William Hardwood, (Harwood) whose family first came to Virginia following the Indian massacre of 1622. Hardwood (Harwood) served as a tobacco inspector, the sheriff of Warwick County and a member of the House of Burgesses before the American Revolution.

The house got its name around 1730 when the direction of the main road leading from Warwick County and Williamsburg to Yorktown was changed so that, instead of running in front, it ran alongside the house.

During the Revolutionary War, Colonial soldiers on the way to Yorktown stopped and camped at "Endview". It is believed that George Washington, whose headquarters was only a mile from "Endview", visited the plantation on several occasions.

Just prior to the Civil War, Humphrey Hardwood (Harwood) Curtis, a cousin of the Hardwoods and one of two doctors in Warwick County, bought Endview. When the war began, Curtis organized the local volunteer company known as the Warwick Beauregards on the front lawn of the property.

During the Warwick River Siege, which was the first phase of the Peninsula Campaign, the house was used as a hospital by Confederate soldiers. When Confederate soldiers retreated from the area, Union soldiers took over the house and also used it as a hospital. The house was used as a temporary headquarters on the day of the Battle of Williamsburg.

The home is a classical colonial structure with several colonial features remaining including the central hallway, the two bays or rooms off the central hallway, both upstairs and downstairs. The two-story structure also has a half basement and its chimneys are made of English bond. The property includes the house, two graveyards and a spring".

Acknowledgment: Gertrude Stead for her research, photographs and transcriptions.

LEBANON CHURCH OF CHRIST

YORKTOWN ROAD (30) {N 3}

History of Church

A group of "Disciples of Christ" (Campbellites) worshiping in the old Episcopal Church called Kiaskiak, separated into two groups. Some of them transferred to Grafton Christian Church in York county, and the rest formed what is now Lebanon Church of Christ. Earliest date of membership is that of Sarah Anne Fox on May 14, 1837.

Description of Graveyard

The graveyard is on the east side and to the rear of the church. There are several family plots, one surrounded by an iron fence has no marks. The earliest grave is 1839. Some Miner Family stones were moved to Lebanon from Fort Eustis (see Mulberry Island Cemeteries).

The cemetery was transcribed by the Works Progress Administration in 1937. The information is available from the *Virginia Historical Inventory (W P A), The Library of Virginia*. Mrs. Gertrude Stead has taken pictures of the tombstones. The following are from pictures.

Capt. Jacob H.
CLEMENTS
Born
Aug. 27, 1830
Died
June 27, 1914
*In thee, O Lord
do I put my trust*
d/s w/ Jennett Lawton

Jennett Lawton
MAYNARD
Wife of
Jacob H. CLEMENTS
Born in Surry Co. Va.
Sept. 7, 1832
Married
June 26, 1856
Died in Warwick
Co. Va. Oct. 30, 1911
d/s w/ Jacob H.

John A. CHARLES
Jan 19, 1852
Feb. 13, 1903

Louisa D. CHARLES
Nov. 25, 1854
April 3, 1898

John C. BEER
Born
Dec. 11, 1844
Died Aug. 1, 1907

Lisetta BEER
wife of
John C. BEER
Born
May 15, 1845
Died
June 13, 1921

Mary CEREZO
March 4, 1858
Feb. 26. 1929

I have Glorified Thee on Earth
I have Finished the Work which
Thou Gavest me to do
Richard Miles
. BRYAN
Born Sept 12, 1845
Died Feb. 22, 1921

Martha Curtis CAMPBELL
November 26, 1872
January 14, 1944

Hugh A. CAMPBELL
May 31, 1862
March 18, 1927

Edward Eugene BRYAN
Nov. 29, 1895
April 30, 1952

Alan Keith CALLIS
US Navy
1946 - 1989

Eddie Samuel BURN
SFC US Army
World War II Korea Vietnan
Nov 26 1926   Jul 17 1990
Headstone (Blackfoot)

Hugh Alexander
CAMPBELL, Jr.
June 24, 1894
Sept. 17, 1965
d/s w/ Claudia Copelan

Claudia Copelan Varn
CAMPBELL
March 12, 1908
d/s w/ Hugh Alexander

Addie Gray CHARLES
Jan. 2, 1882
Oct. 2, 1888

Betty Page CHARLES
March 20, 1923
July 28, 1976

J. Allen CHARLES
July 2, 1880
Oct. 12, 1952

J. Henry CHARLES
April 26, 1878
Oct. 25, 1946

Maud B. CHARLES
Aug. 26, 1886
March 2, 1954

Wm. J. CHARLES
Died Oct. 20, 1934
Age 62 Yrs.
At Rest

George Durbin
CHENOWETH
1847 - 1930
d/s w/ Emma Leake

Emma Leake
CHENOWETH
1861 - 1951
d/s w/ George Durbin

Ashton W. CLARKE
Aug. 16, 1895
Feb. 5, 1951

Nannie Read CLARKE
Dec. 25, 1902
Oct. 20, 1984

Thomas F.
CLEMENTS
Born
Jan. 15, 1867
Died
July 4, 1923
Asleep in Jesus

Alice Minson COOKE
Consort of
Dr. S. G. COOKE
went to rest
Jan. 24, 1936

Dr. Stafford G. COOKE
Born in York Co. Va.
Dec. 1, 1860
Died
Mar. 2, 1937

Dorothy Saxby COOKE
Born
Feb. 13, 1902
Died
Feb. 16, 1994

S. Minson COOKE
Born
July 1, 1897
Died
Feb. 25, 1955

Andrew C. CRAFFORD
June 29, 1888
Sept. 5, 1978

Carter CRAFFORD
June 2, 1882
Sept. 30, 1967

Edward T. CRAFFORD
Feb. 24, 1876
Feb. 25, 1917

Helen M. CRAFFORD
May 26, 1880
Sept. 17, 1964
Founder
Zeta Tau Alpha

CRAFFORD

Dr. John CRAFFORD
Wife
Eva Salter CRAFFORD

John C. CRAFFORD
Aug. 19, 1916
Feb. 20, 1917

John E. CRAFFORD
Feb. 16, 1886
Oct. 1, 1957

Infant Daughter of
Dr. M. V. & M. Josephine
CRAFFORD
Born Jan 6, 1912

Lucy L. CRAFFORD
Oct. 3, 1873
July 6, 1958

The following four are
on an Obelisk stone

Wm. CRAFFORD son of
Wm. C. CRAFFORD &
Mary Waller CRAFFORD
Born May 14, 1845
Died Mch. 24, 1889

Emma V. CRAFFORD
Daughter of
Wm. & Lucy CRAFFORD
Born Oct 16, 1877
Died Feb. 10, 1899

Henry V. CRAFFORD
son of
Wm. & Lucy CRAFFORD
Born July 6, 1870
Died Jan. 14, 1908

Annie C. CRAFFORD
Daughter of
Wm. & Lucy CRAFFORD
Born Mch. 3, 1862
Died Feb. 5, 1887

Next four are on same stone

Sarah E. CRAFFORD
Daughter of
Wm. & Lucy CRAFFORD
Born May 11, 1876
Died Feb. 11, 1871

M. Alice CRAFFORD
daughter of
Wm. & Lucy CRAFFORD
Born Mch. 8, 1879
Died April 17, 1881

V. Adora CRAFFORD
Daughter of
Born April 4, 1880
Died April 21, 1881

Infant son of
Wm. & Lucy CRAFFORD
Born Dec. 12, 1867

Lucy A. CRAFFORD
wife of
Wm. CRAFFORD
Daughter of
Carter CRAFFORD
and
Lucy Harwood
CRAFFORD
Born
Oct. 24, 1845
Died
Dec. 3, 1919

William C. CRAFFORD
Feb. 4, 1873
Nov. 11, 1951

Annie Sims CURTIS
June 4, 1904
January 5, 1988

Carter Coleman CURTIS
August 31, 1894
June 27, 1962

Christopher C. CURTIS
Nov. 7, 1890
Sept. 18, 1952

Corinne B. CURTIS
Nov. 16, 1925
Nov. 14, 1943
Only Asleep

Edith Pitts CURTIS
August 27, 1897
February 4, 1992

Douglas Cary CURTIS Sr.
April 16, 1896
August 30, 1978

Douglas Cary CURTIS Jr.
April 25, 1939
September 7, 1992

Elizabeth Read CURTIS
Aug. 31, 1873
April 3, 1937

Emma Chewning CURTIS
Sept. 8, 1872
Dec. 2, 1960

Frances Cary CURTIS
June 27, 1865
July 8, 1935

Lloyd E. CURTIS
Oct. 24, 1896
Mar. 18, 1957

Lloyd Elton CURTIS
CPL. US Army
Korea
Oct. 23, 1932 May 30, 1981

Maria E. Whitaker CURTIS
Sept. 1, 1836
May 19, 1919

Mary Lee CURTIS
Born Feby. 15, 1834
Died Feby. 7, 1916
Aged 82 Years
At Rest

Minnie F. Shawver
CURTIS
Dec. 25, 1880
Nov. 30, 1945

Nevada B. CURTIS
Jan. 19, 1900
Apr. 11, 1978

Robert Thomas CURTIS
Jan. 18, 1870
Dec. 20, 1932

Nannie L. Cooke CURTIS
Feb. 28, 1864
Dec. 9, 1947

Simon C. CURTIS
Capt US Army
Jun. 13, 1910
Feb. 12, 1986

Simon Reid CURTIS
June 16, 1863
Aug. 4, 1949
Treasurer of Warwick County 45 years

Ralph Edwards
son of
L. S. & C. M. DAMAN
1928 - 1930
Asleep in Jesus

In Memory of
Joaquin Robert De VIGNIER
1917 - 1976
Husband of
Helen Harwood De VIGNIER

Lulie Harwood DUNN
July 9, 1879 Aug. 24, 1929
d/s w/ John

John DUNN
Feb. 21, 1867 - Nov. 16, 1932
d/s w/ Lulie Harwood

Preston T. EPPERSON
PFC US Army
Korea
Mar. 22, 1919 Apr. 18, 1983

Robert Coleman EPPERSON
April 10, 1910
July 3, 1960

Ruby Steele EPPERSON
January 22, 1914
June 6, 1958

Mary C. FOX
Feb. 22, 1878
Oct. 16, 1918

Infant Dau of
J. W. & Anna
FLETCHER
Born & Died
Jan 8, 1921
Gone but not forgotten

Janet Rae FLETCHER
Daughter of
Mr. & Mrs. E. C. FLETCHER
Born Sept. 14, 1934
Stone sunken in ground

Robert M. FLETCHER
Apr. 11, 1913
Nov. 18, 1988
d/s w/ Pircy C.

Pircy C. FLETCHER
June 25, 1913
Apr. 3, 1986
d/s w/ Robert M.

Robert Murcher
FLETCHER
July 30, 1937
March 10, 1959
Asleep in Jesus
Picture on stone

Martha Fannie
wife of
T. H. FLEMING
Feb. 1. 1897
Oct. 9, 1918
Faithful to her trust
even unto death
d/s w/ Thomas Hayes

Thomas Hayes
FLEMING
Oct. 26, 1882
Sept. 29, 1945
d/s w/ Martha Fannie

Kenneth M. GOULD
1906 - 1994
d/s w/ Dorothea T.

Dorothea T. GOULD
1910 -
d/s w/ Kenneth M.

Alexander Gilliam HARWOOD III
Born
September 19, 1912
Died
March 9, 1945
In the Service of his Country
Father in thy Gracious keeping
leave us now thy servant sleeping

George Montgomery HARWOOD
January 13, 1888
September 18, 1952
Softly now the light of day
fades upon my sights away

George Washington
HARWOOD
Born Feb. 24, 1860
Died March 11, 1918

Indiana Virginia HARWOOD
Born Apr. 16, 1836
Died Oct. 6, 1906
Peace Perfect Peace

L. G. HARWOOD
Born
Mch. 11, 1867
Died
Apr. 22, 1908

E. C. HARWOOD
Born April 14, 1830
Died
Feb. 21, 1886
How sweet to look in thoughtful hope
Beyond the Fading Sky
And hear Him call His Children
up to His fair home on high.

W. A. Sammy HOGGE
1918 - 1983
d/s w/ Laura M.

Laura M. HOGGE
1916 -
d/s w/ W. A. Sammy

Ethel Julia HOOD
1896 - 1949
d/s w/ James Ralph

James Ralph HOOD
1896 -
d/s w/ Ethel Julia
Just away

Henry L. HORN
PFC US Army
World War II
Oct. 7, 1920   Apr. 19, 1991
Father

Beloved Wife and Mother
Mary Epperson HORN
July 24, 1921 - Feb. 3, 1975

Willie J. HORN
Sept. 22, 1889
May 1, 1972

Helen M. HORNSBY
June 28, 1904
Nov. 17, 1983

Mollie Weymouth
HURLEY
June 22, 1860
Aug. 18, 1930

Sarah
Beloved Wife of
T. C. HUTCHINS
Died April 2, 1920
Age 51 Yrs.

Elsie Epperson JOHNSON
January 21, 1908
April 28, 1954

Floyd Wilmer JOHNSON, Sr.
December 24, 1903
August 14, 1972

Wm. A. JONES
York Co. Va.
1850 - 1906
At Rest

Eva M. JORDAN
April 23, 1923
Jan. 8, 1925

Lucy B. JORDAN
April 23, 1923
April 24, 1923

Banister P. KIRBY
Feb. 12, 1855
Apr. 19, 1905
*Lifes Work Well Done
He Rests in Peace.*

Calie D. KIRBY
Feb. 7, 1860
Aug. 10, 1895
*A Devoted Wife
and Mother*

Our Darling
Cora B. KIRBY
Feb. 20, 1916
June 4, 1917

In loving memory of
Earl Lee KIRBY Sr.
Nov. 8, 1917
Dec. 24, 1990

Elizabeth KIRBY
May 18, 1882
July 15, 1912
*She is not Dead
but sleeping*

Our Darling
Harwood KIRBY
June 4, 1895
Sept. 6, 1896

Irene Curtis KIRBY
Oct. 17, 1869
Feb. 27, 1936

Jack KIRBY
Jan. 7, 1884
Apr. 2, 1971

Josephine Maude KIRBY
Sept. 5, 1900
Feb. 22, 1971
Marker VFW Ladies Auxiliary

Julia V. KIRBY
Mar. I, 1886
Aug. 22, 1928
*A Devoted Wife
and Mother*

William H. KIRBY
May 22, 1866
Aug. 28, 1942

William P. KIRBY III
March 1, 1942
Sept. 7, 1942

William P. KIRBY Jr.
Feb. 27, 1922
June 9, 1955

William P. KIRBY Sr.
Sept. 20, 1888
Sept. 28, 1965

Vernon W. KIRBY
March 17, 1908
Dec. 1, 1962

Mary Anna Kirby
KNAUFF
Sept. 21, 1898
Jan. 7, 1978

Edna B. LEE
Sept. 1876
Dec. 1950

Frank LEE
Jan 9, 1896
July 30, 1972
d/s w/ Myrtle E.

Myrtle E. LEE
Oct. 4, 1894
Feb. 14, 1969
d/s w/ Frank
Gone but not Forgotten

Son
Lester C. LUSBY
1900 - 1949

Johnnie Mae MARSHALL
June 30, 1906
Jan. 22, 1955

M. Cecil MESSICK
July 21, 1907
June 25, 1991
d/s w/ Frances W.

Frances W. MESSICK
Mar. 19, 1908
May 15, 1991

May Dozier MESSICK
1880 - 1967

Mary Treslyn MESSICK
Feb. 23, 1912
Aug. 20, 1933
Only Asleep

Emmett Ward MILSTEAD
1859 - 1932
d/s w/ Nannie Wynne

Nannie Wynne MILSTEAD
1862 - 1932
d/s w/ Emmett Ward

In memory of my sister
Ann Eliza MINER
daughter of
S. H. & S. L. MINER
Born Oct. 25, 1835
Died Oct. 22, 1839

In memory of my wife
Mary MINER
Daughter of
Carter and Lucy CRAFFORD
Wife of
Wm. Christopher MINER
Born Nov. 19, 1846
Died Feb. 28, 1898
A Loving True and Perfect Wife
My Hope & Joy of this Earthy Life
By the will of one who Doeth All
In Heaven with thee I Hope
to Dwell

Henry C. MINER
Aug. 29, 1877
Sept. 20, 1934

In memory of my Brother
Sam'l Hyde MINER
son of
S. H. & S. L. MINER
Born Dec. 20, 1842
Died Apr. 20, 1866

Samuel H. MINER
CPL 32nd Va. Infantry CSA
Dec. 20, 1842 Apr. 20, 1866

In memory of
our Father
William C. MINER

Son of S. H. & Sarah L. MINER
Husband of
Mary CRAFFORD
Born Columbus, Ohio
July 10, 1838
Died Dec. 25, 1914

William C. MINER
1 Lieut 32 Va. Inf. CSA
July 10, 1839 Dec. 25, 1914

William C. MINER Jr.
Nov. 2, 1870
Oct. 2, 1921

Winslow H. MINER
Sept. 11, 1872
Feb. 12, 1937

In Memory of My Mother
Sarah Langley HABBELL
Formerly wife of
Sam'l H. MINER
Daughter of
Wm. & Elizabeth HARWOOD
Born Oct. 2, 1814
Died April 4, 1888

In memory of my Son
Sam'l Carter MINER
son of
W. C. & Mary MINER
Born June 28, 1867
Died Sept. 16, 1896

In memory of my Father
Sam'l Hyde MINER
son of
Christopher & Matilda
MINER
Born Aug. 1, 1801
Died Sept. 16, 1843

Folmer H. MOLLER Jr.
Aug. 4, 1921
Dec. 30, 1927

Helen B. MOLLER
Oct. 13, 1923
Dec. 14, 1923

Joseph Samuel MOORE
Nov. 3, 1855
April 26, 1926

Ralph Haywood MOORE
July 7, 1892
Oct. 25, 1963

Warner F.
son of
F. M. & W. F. MOORE Jr.
Oct. 10, 1842
Oct. 18, 1842
Asleep in Jesus

Edward Filmore NETTLES
July 20, 1867
d/s w/ Mary Crafford

Mary Crafford NETTLES
May 1, 1872
Nov. 19, 1929
d/s w/ Edward Filmore

Ernest L.
Beloved son of
Omer and Janie
PARRISH
Born Nov. 8, 1922
Died Aug. 28, 1928

John Bertram REED
Sept. 7, 1897
April 27, 1961
Military marker
John Bertram REED
Ohio
CPL Quartermaster Corps
World War 1
Sept. 7, 1897 April 27, 1961

Laura Virginia REED
Feb. 27, 1894
Aug. 5, 1980

Addie L. McGuire
RICHARDSON
Oct. 21, 1877
June 28, 1947

Allen Dawson
RICHARDSON
Oct. 19, 1881
Sept. 19, 1962

Abraham RIGGLE
Born
Feb. 5, 1833
Died
Oct. 30, 1911

Daisy M. RIGGLE
Jan. 1865
Nov. 1913

Earl A. RIGGLE
Georgia
PVT Infantry
Nov. 8, 1890 May 15, 1964

Alexina S. RIPLEY
1856 - 1935
d/s w/ George W.

George W. RIPLEY Sr.
1849 - 1926
d/s w/ Alexina S.

Father
Coleman F. RIPLEY
Sept. 21, 1911
Jan. 23, 1981
At Rest

Clyde H. RIPLEY
1918 - 1918

Douglas C. RIPLEY
1916 - 1918

Frank LEE
Jan. 9, 1896
July 30, 1972
d/s w/ Myrtle E.

Myrtle E. LEE
Oct. 4. 1894
Feb. 14, 1969
Gone but not Forgotten
d/s w/ Frank

RIPLEY
Ella
Virginia
Rebecca
Alexina "Lady" SMITH

George RIPLEY
1881 - 1960
d/s w/ Mary A.

Mary A. RIPLEY
1883 - 1958
d/s w/ George

Father
Harry C. RIPLEY
Nov. 1, 1906
May 24, 1984
d/s w/ Beatrice

Mother
Beatrice RIPLEY
May 23, 1905
Aug. 6, 1989
d/s w/ Harry C.

James A. RIPLEY
1883 - 1926

Mother
Mattie I. RIPLEY
Aug. 9, 1887
June 4, 1945

Mother
Nellie B. RIPLEY
Nov. 17, 1920
Oct. 4, 1971

Father
James C. RIPLEY
Oct. 25, 1905
Jan. 24, 1929

Father
Coleman F. RILEY
Sept. 11, 1911
Jan. 23, 1981
At Rest

Mother
Nellie B. KIRBY
Nov. 17, 1920
Oct. 4, 1971

Noble E. ROBERTS
Sept. 23, 1923
Dec. 15, 1984

Robert L. ROBERTS, Jr.
Aug. 29, 1972
Sept. 15, 1972

Alice
Wife of
J. B. SAVAGE
Born July 10, 1885
Died
Aug. 30, 1907

Julia Faye
SAWYER
1911 - 1992

William Lee SAWYER
1887 - 1946
d/s w/ Alice Skillman

Alice Skillman SAWYER
1889 - 1960
d/s w/ William Lee

Clara Estelle
SCHELL
July 7, 1880
Feb. 5, 1920
*She was the Sunshine
of our Home*

Frederick SCHMIDT
Died June 10, 1914
Aged 73 Years

Oliver R. SCOTT
1881 - 1953

Birdie Aphia
wife of
D. S. SHEPHERD
Nov. 23, 1864
Oct. 11, 1912
Peace Perfect Peace

D. S. SHEPHERD
Born
June 21, 1856
Died
Dec. 11, 1900
*Blessed Are Those
who die in the Lord.*

Alice Nelson COOKE
Wife of
J. H. SATTERFIELD
Dec. 2, 1900
Mar. 13, 1934

James H. SATTERFIELD
US Marine Corps
World War 1 & 11
Jul. 27, 1892   Oct. 1, 1976

Tom
John Archer SHEILD
October 20, 1889
July 15, 1945

Sally Cooke SHEILD
Died
March 16, 1954

In Loving Memory
of Our Father
Benjamin R.
SKILLMAN
Feb. 2, 1849
Jan 13, 1935

G. Gilbert
SKILLMAN
July 10, 1895
Jan. 14, 1940

Julia A. SKILLMAN
Born
Sept. 3, 1891
Died
Aug 7, 1907
At Rest

*In Loving Memory
of our Mother*
Sara Williams
SKILLMAN
June 6, 1861
Dec. 8, 1951

Milan SMITH
1837 - 1913
His wife
Lucinda SMITH
1842 - 1897
*Gone but not
Forgotten*

Daniel J. SWANSON
Dec. 9, 1973
Dec. 11, 1973

Nancy C. SWEENEY
Aug. 21, 1927
Aug. 24, 1982

Frederick H. TENNIS
Virginia
PVT CO D 3 Engr Trg Regt
World War 1
April 15, 1892   June 17, 1957

R. Fitchett TENNIS
1903 - 1952

Lillian FITCHETT
Wife of
F. L. TENNIS
Jan. 27, 1869
Apr. 30, 1938
A tender mother and a faithful friend

Frederick Lee
TENNIS
Jan. 23. 1864
Mar. 22. 1946
A faithful Father and a true friend

Son
Frank D. TERRELL
Sept. 10   Jan. 22
1962   1986

J. T. THACKER
Aug. 10, 1849
Nov. 9, 1926

Leo S. WAGONER
Feb. 14, 1915
Dec. 10, 1982

James Willard WAID
March 14, 1919
March 14, 1974

Emma C. WALSH
Jan. 31. 1882
Mar. 15, 1956

Sussannah M. Newman
WALKER
Sept. 30, 1829
Sept. 1, 1905

Leroy C. WALSH
Oct. 30, 1889
Feb. 9, 1934

Anna Mary WEST
May 8, 1852
Sept. 9, 1923

Alexander D. WEST
April 9, 1848
Oct. 19, 1916

Samuel K. WEST
Aug. 2, 1827
Oct. 1, 1931

Virginia K. WEST
Aug. 25, 1877
Aug. 13, 1956

William C. WHITAKER
July 7, 1838
Jan 2, 1919

Mary V. WILLIAMS
1939 - 1939

Nannie Curtis WILLIAMSON
Jan. 25, 1881 - Nov. 8, 1943
d/s w/ James C.

James C. WILLIAMSON
Feb. 26, 1876 - Sept. 6, 1946
d/s w/ Nannie Curtis

Charles G. WILLIS
North Carolina
P2 USNRF
World War 1
Jan. 2, 1898 - April 29, 1954

Bettie
Wife of
J. T. WOOTEN
Born June 3, 1851
Died
April 29, 1908

John T.
WOOTEN Jr.
Born May 26, 1887
Died June 17, 1906
Marker by VFW Ladies Auxiliary

Mary D.
WOOTEN
June 9, 1861
March 5, 1926
Asleep in Jesus

Baker P. WYNNE
July 6, 1874
July 28, 1951

Effie Cary WYNNE
July 6, 1874
Jan. 24, 1969

Hannah Mahala WYNNE
March 15, 1871
Jan. 12, 1966

Miles Wills WYNNE
Dec. 30, 1876
April 26, 1961

Nina V. WYNNE
Feb. 14, 1869
March 12, 1950

Robert Baker WYNNE
March 27, 1906
Dec. 10, 1970

In sacred remembrance of our
beloved Father
Elder Tho. G. WYNNE
Born Aug. 25, 1834
Died Sept. 15, 1904
I have fought a good fight
I have finished my course
I have kept the faith
Hence forth there is laid up
For me a crown of righteousness
Which the Lord the righteous
Judge shall give me in that day

Wm. B. WYNNE
Born
Aug. 20, 1832
Died
Feb. 9, 1922

Bettie H. WYNNE
Born
May 7, 1844
Died
July 10, 1922

Junior Clay
YEAGER
April 5, 1918
March 16, 1969

Avis Dale
YEAGER
Jan. 20, 1926
Jan. 1, 1967

Father
George Edward BRYAN
Born Jan. 11, 1854
Died May 18, 1914
*I have fought a good fight
I have finished the course
I have kept the faith.*

Rogert T.
WYNNE
Oct. 6. 1853
March 16, 1926

The following tombstone was on the 1937 (W P A) list but was not on the Gertrude Stead 1996 transcriptions. The following is from the (W P A) records.

Mother
Irodeen Harwood BRYAN
Born July 7, 1857
Died November 27, 1940
*Peace I leave with you
my peace I give unto you*

Acknowledgment: Gertrude Stead for research, transcriptions and photographs.

The Lebanon Christian Church Cemetery

The Lebanon Christian Church Cemetery

The Lebanon Christian Church Cemetery

LEE GRAVEYARD

CURTIS ROAD (15) {M 6}

This Lee graveyard is the family burying ground of the Lees of the "Lee Hall" estate. "Lee Hall" was established in early 1700, and this graveyard had its beginning a few years later.

The following is from the *Virginia Historical Inventory, (W P A), The Library of Virginia*. The information in {} was transcribed by F. W. Boelt in January 1994.

OBELISK 3 NAMES

R. Lee DAVIS
1851 - 1925

Angie L. DAVIS
1843 - 1881

{Frances L. DAVIS
1862 - 1956}

OBELISK 3 NAMES

Father & Mother
Allen DAVIS
1804 - 1874

Sarah E. DAVIS
1822 - 1879
Grandfather & Mother
Robert H. LEE
& Wife

OBELISK 3 NAMES

Robert Lewis DAVIS
1838 - Killed
C.S.A. 1865

M. T.{J.} HOPKINS
1840 - 1901

W. G. DAVIS
1853 - 1881

OBELISK 3 NAMES

R. D. LEE
Born Jan. 28, 1821
{Jan. 21, 1821}
Died June 7, 1896

E. T. LEE
Born Febru. 13, 1847
Died May 12, 1905

Martha E. LEE
Born May 8, 1822
{Born May 7, 1822}
Died April 15, 1877

{Richard L. DAVIS Jr.
May 14, 1885
Dec 20, 1964}

{Hazel Priece DAVIS
Aug. 2, 1888
May 23, 1984}

{John H. YOUNG
1843 - 1914}

{Allen DAVIS
Born July 11, 1867
Died Dec 23 18??}

{Allen & Sarah DAVIS
Born July 21, 1853
Died May 20, 185?}

Angie
Beloved wife of
R. Lee DAVIS
and daughter of Wm. & A. LEE
was born Oct. 1, 1845
And died a consistent & devoted
Member of "Lebanon Church"
May 6, 1881
"Sad is the house and lone the hours
Since thy sweet smiles are gone.
But Oh! A brighter home than ours
In heaven is now thine own"

William H.
Son of Allen and Sarah E. DAVIS
Born July 31, 1853
Died may 30, 1881
Ah, when at death we part
How deep now keen the pain
But we shall still be joined in heart
And hope to meet again

Allen DAVIS
Born July 14, 1804
Died Dec. 26, 1874
Upon thy Grave shall Blessings rest
Kind, good and gentle were thy ways,
Thy loved the most who have the best
And thy affections speak thy praise

Acknowledgment: Gertrude Stead visited and photographed the site and noted the following;
There are two obelisk stones, four flat stones, one foot stone with no head stone and three stones leaning against a tree and against one of the obelisk stones. Other stones lying on the ground have no inscriptions.

Allen Davis 1804 - 1874

Robert Lewis Davis, Killed 1865

MANEY CEMETERY
MAIN STREET AND MANEY DRIVE (10) {J 37}

Maney Cemetery

This cemetery is located on the property, that was the Maney Farm.

Alice R. MANEY
Entered into Rest
May 6, 1917
Asleep in Jesus blessed sleep
From which none ever wake to
keep. A calm and undisturbed
repose. Unbroken by the last of foes.

Mallory
MANEY
Oct. 16, 1852
May 21, 1920
Gone but not Forgotten

BUTLER
Archie   Emily
1890-1981   1895-1970

Annie Louise
Daughter of
Robt and Mattie WILSON
Born July 15, 1913
Died Oct. 20, 1918

Father
Thomas David
LYLISTON
Feb. 19, 1869
Nov. 12, 1911

Mother
Susie M. ASKEW
Wife of
Cleveland L. BERRY
and John I. ASKEW
1892 - 1957

Father
Cleveland L. BERRY
1882 - 1943

Stone vase in a enclosed
area. No names

Samuel D. Y. GALLATIN
1882 - 1940

William N. HUBBARD
Oct. 21, 1893
Oct. 16, 1956

Frances N. HUBBARD
Jan. 1, 1903
July 5, 1988

Father
Robert W. WYATT
Sept. 27, 1873
March 2, 1944
Asleep in Jesus

Mother
Mary S. WYATT
Wife of
Robert W. WATSON
May 8, 1877
May 1, 1929

Infant son of
Stephen & E. A. TURNER
Born
Sept. 1, 1896
Died
July 23, 1897
Our darling baby

Infant son of
Stephen &
E. A. TURNER
Born
Aug. 1, 1894
Died
Oct. 23, 1894
Our darling baby

Mother
Elizabeth Anne TURNER
1866 - 1932

Father
Stephen TURNER
1865 - 1934

William H. TURNER
1857 - 1935

HAHNN
Virginia HAHNN
Sept.. 21, 1936
June 3, 1957
Sheltered and safe
from sorrow

Winfred L. SAUNDERS
Jan. 15, 1914
Sept. 14, 1948
Foot stone - Mother

Thomas L. SAUNDERS
Feb. 16, 1868
April 24, 1943
Foot stone - Father

Laura J. SAUNDERS
Aug. 8, 1861
Sept. 29, 1934
Foot stone - Mother

Richard LYLISTON
born
Nov. 27, 1840
died
Nov. 14. 1903
Age 63 years

Martha Susan LYLISTON
Born
Apr. 12. 1839
Died
Oct. 16, 1910

Father
Thomas David LYLISTON
Feb. 19, 1869
Nov. 12, 1911

William Henry Clay
LYLISTON
Born Dec. 30, 1876
Died March 10, 1919
At rest

Carrie B. LYLISTON
Born Feb. 20, 1879
Died July 7, 1919
Dear wife I hope to meet you
when life pilgrimage is oer.
For I can see your face so sweetly
Shining on the other shore.

Richard J. LYLISTON
Born Oct. 11, 1873
Died Oct. 9, 1930

Ann Bachelor
LYLISTON
Born
Nov. 21, 1820
Died
Oct. 16, 1882

David LYLISTON
Born
Aug. 9, 1810
Died
Apr. 23. 1881

Julia Etta LUERSSEN
May 29, 1876
Dec. 26, 1951

Frank B. LUERSSEN
Born
May 28, 1900
Died
Aug 11, 1900

Baby LUERSSEN
Born
Aug. 26, 1901
Died Sept. 1901

Julia E. LUERSSEN
Born
July 16, 1905
Died
Aug. 17, 1906

George LUERSSEN
Mar. 7, 1865
Apr. 15, 1942

Maud H.
SAUNDERS
Born
May 9, 1872
Died
Oct. 18, 1873

William B.
SAUNDERS
Born
Jan 4, 1874
Died Jan. 21, 1874

Sarah A. SAUNDERS
Born
June 20, 1835
Died
Dec. 30, 1879

William Wesley SAUNDERS
Born Dec. 28, 1879
Died Nov. 4, 1927
Foot stone - W.W.S.

Thomas L. MANEY
Feb. 18, 1874
Jan. 21, 1942

Burckett MANEY
Dec. 20, 1896
Oct. 24, 1968

(Double stone)
MATER
Rosa   Jake
Jan. 28, 1888   Dec. 9, 1886
Feb. 27, 1961   Jan. 22, 1933

George D. WILSON
Nov. 10, 1899
Dec. 1, 1929

Clara Virginia
MITCHELL
Born Sept. 17, 1857
Died March 30, 1930
At Rest

Thomas B. MITCHELL
Born Dec. 31. 1896
Died Nov. 2, 1926
An earthly sunbeams
vanished;
Radiant still the sky

Thomas SAUNDERS
Jan. 28, 1859
Jan. 5, 1930

Lillie SAUNDERS
April 3, 1869
March 26, 1964

Father	Mother
Richard WILSON	Maria L. WILSON
Husband of	Wife of
M. L. WILSON	Richard WILSON
Born	Born
April 1, 1848	Aug. 16, 1860
Died	Died
Oct. 12, 1906	Dec. 31, 1930

(Tall marble shaft with father's name on one side, mother's name on the other side)

Wilton J. WILSON
Oct. 25, 1897
May 12, 1922

Walker W. WILSON
Sept. 16, 1890
Dec. 9, 1963

Father
John Alfronza BAINES
May 29, 1868
Sept. 27, 1951
At rest

Mother
Zelia Ann BAINES
Jan. 28, 1872
Dec. 8, 1936
Live for Jesus

S. Joseph
son of
J. A. & Z. A.
BAINES
Born
Sept. 24, 1895
Died
June 12, 1896

Mary Zella POWELL
May 28, 1919
April 30, 1938

(Double stone)
MANEY

Stephen	Ann P.
1849-1899	1853-1933

Allie G.
Son of
S. & A. P. MANEY
Born
Apr. 29, 1880
Died
Dec. 1, 1885

Roland L.
Son of S. R. &
Clara MANEY
Jan. 19, 1907
Dec. 22, 1907

Large Double stone with
just the word "MANEY"
Stephen R.
Hayes MANEY
Feb. 14, 1877
Nov. 20, 1959
Foot stone

Clara L. MANEY
Wife of S. R. MANEY
July 11, 1876
Sept. 5, 1944
Foot stone

Acknowledgment: Gertrude Stead for taking pictures and doing transcriptions. Mr. Paul Brown for transcribing tombstones, from *Tidewater Genealogical Quarterly* Vol. 20, No.2, June 1989.

Mallory Maney

MILES CARY 1 CEMETERY

OWENS DRIVE (14) {G 17}

The following is from the *Virginia Historical Inventory, (W P A), The Library of Virginia*.

The family burying ground of Miles CARY, the immigrant, is situated on a high bluff overlooking Lucas Creek. It is not far from the site of the home of the CARYS. There is only one tomb, the one of Miles CARY, which is a large slab resting on a brick foundation of a foot and a half in height. This tomb was remodeled by the Colonial Daughters a few years ago. They filled in some of the missing pieces and made the brick foundation. They also placed an iron fence around the tomb. One large walnut tree stands at the head of the tomb. Several old bricks can be seen pushing their way up through the roots of the tree, so there must have been other tombs in this graveyard at one time.

HISTORICAL SIGNIFICANCE:

This graveyard is of great historical interest because the first CARY who came to this part of the country was buried in this little cemetery. He was the ancestor of all the CARYS who were so important in the affairs of the county later.

The following is the inscription on the tomb of Miles CARY;

> Here lyeth the Body of Miles CARY ESQ
> only son of John CARY & Alice his wife
> Daughter of Henry HOBSON of the City of
> Bristol, Alderman. He was born in Said City
> And departed this life on 10th Day of June 1667
> About the 47th year of his Age leaving four
> Sons and three daughters Thomas
> Jane Henry Brigette Elizabeth
> Miles & William
> (Remodelled by Colonial Daughters)

Acknowledgment: Gertrude Stead for the research and photographs.

Miles Cary 1

MILES CARY CEMETERY AT RICHNECK

RICHNECK ROAD (13) {M 15}
McINTOSH SCHOOL

The following is form the *Virginia Historical Inventory, (W P A), The Library of Virginia*, recorded by Dorothy Diffenderfer on 5 April 1937.

"This graveyard, when the property of the Carys, was surrounded by a well built brick wall with a coping, and contained a number of stones marking the graves of members of the Cary family. The wall has long since been removed to build foundations of houses.

By the irony of fate, Captain James Moody removed and destroyed the gravestones of Richneck burying ground because he did not win the hand of the lovely widow, Mary Roscow, who later married Miles Cary. Only the stone of Miles Cary and his first wife, Mary Milner, was spared. It was broken into fragments but has been cemented together and placed on a brick base. It was restored by Thomas Nelson, Jr. Chapter, *Sons of the American Revolution*, a few years ago.

Tradition:

Among the many traditions handed down from father to son, none could be of more interest than the "*Old Elm*", under whose shade the first courts of Warwick County were held. In Colonial Days, the "*Court Elm*" stood in the old Cary cemetery at Richneck as a silent guard over the graves of those who helped to make the history of Warwick County.

> Here lyeth ye Body of Mary the wife
> of Miles CARY & Daughter of Thomas
> MILNER and Mary his wife late of
> Nanzemond county dec'd. She was
> Born the 6th of August 1667 and Died
> the 27th of October 1700 in the 34th
> year of her Age. Issuelefs
> Alfo the Body of Col. Miles CARY
> Husband of the said Mary who
> died February 17th 1708 & left 2 Sons
> Wilson & Miles & 2 daughters
> Mary & Ann by Mary ye Daughter
> of Col. Wm. WILSON of Hampton"

From the *Daily Press, March 11, 1983*;

NEWPORT NEWS - "The grave of Miles Cary II, a prominent Colonial settler, now has a new marker, thanks to the city's Historical Committee and Department of Parks and Recreation. The tombstone, reconstructed after vandals had destroyed the original, was dedicated

Thursday at the grave site of Cary and his wife, Mary, under the "*Charter Elm*" pictured on the seal of the City of Newport News.

About 80 people attended the ceremony, including Cary Morton, 13, of Newport News, a Cary descendant. The Walsingham Academy student unveiled the marker.

The tombstone is on the grounds of the George J. McIntosh Elementary School. In the 17th century, the land was part of a Cary family plantation. Remains of the house are in the fenced-in area behind the school.

An archaeological dig seven years ago by high school students, working under a federal grant, turned up a number of artifacts, but was stopped when money ran out.

Cary, who lived from 1655 to 1708, was a member of the House of Burgesses and commissioner and clerk of the court of Warwick County.

While living at the Richneck Plantation, willed to him by his father who settled large portions of upper Newport News, Cary frequently entertained the court at his home and also maintained the clerk's office there.

In the summer, commissioners are said to have gathered under the shade of a huge elm tree to carry on the county business.

In reconstructing the tombstone, the city's parks department copied the Colonial way of putting together brick and mortar. The inscription on the granite slab, shipped from England by the historical committee, is the same as the original, although one of Cary's descendants remembers a coat of arms also being on the tombstone.

Cary's mother, Mrs. Richard W. Morton, said the inscription in Latin meant "Without God we are nothing."

Miles Cary I, the original settler who died in 1667, is buried on Owens Drive along Warwick River, the site of the 17th-century Windmill Point Plantation, which also belonged to the family.

The state chapter of the Children of the American Revolution plans to place a showcase at the Richneck site this year."

Miles Cary II and Wife, Mary Milner Cary

Acknowledgment: Gertrude Stead visited the site, took pictures and researched the information.

MULBERRY ISLAND CEMETERIES

FORT EUSTIS

An important aspect of the history of Mulberry Island, the site of present day Fort Eustis, is the location and identification of the cemeteries, some in use for several centuries. Unfortunately, any discussion of the former burial sites on Mulberry Island must leave many questions unanswered. Numerous details, such as names, dates and places are incomplete or missing altogether. It is probable that the earliest inhabitants - the Indians - lived, died and were buried here, but where? The answer to this question may never be known.

More is known about the white and black inhabitants, but not nearly enough. Both white men and black men have lived on this so-called island (Part of Stanley Hundred) for about 350 years. In 1622, an Indian massacre almost annihilated the new Colony. John Rolfe, who married Pocahantas and later planted tobacco on Mulberry island, died here about that time, possibly a victim of the massacre, although some authorities disagree. Undoubtedly, the victims of the massacre were buried near their homes.

Although there was a church established on the island by 1627, Mulberry Island families frequently had their own burial grounds. In 1918, when the Army obtained the land, it offered assistance and gave the families on the island 30 days in which to relocate their dead from the existing plots. Some of the families did so, with reburials taking place at Lebanon Church Cemetery in Lee Hall and in other nearby cemeteries.

In the agricultural economy of 1610 to 1918, tombstones and grave markers were expensive and difficult to move into remote areas such as Mulberry Island. Consequently, most graves were marked, if at all, with wooden headboards or crosses which did not survive the passage of time. Some graves were marked by planting flowers or trees at the head or foot of the graves, or both. Frequently, still thriving periwinkle, planted for remembrance, marks an early grave site.

OLD FAMILY CEMETERIES

There are nine definitely known family plots where burials took place prior to 1918 when the Army obtained the property. Most of the known plots have been identified by elderly members of such families as the CRAFFORDS and NETTLES, who lived in the area at that time.

The following Mulberry Island Cemeteries information is from the *Virginia Historical Inventory, (W P A), The Library of Virginia*, recorded in 1937 and a research paper from the *Fort Eustis Historical and Archaeological Association*, by Col. Jean M. Gray, AUS, Retired.

CARTER CRAFFORD FAMILY CEMETERY
(40) {E 11}

This cemetery is located a few feet from the maintenance road adjacent to and southwest of the golf course maintenance shop at Fort Eustis. It contains 24 graves. Eight were members of the CRAFFORD family; ten others were members of the ADAMS, NETTLES and SMITH families. The remaining six graves are unidentified. The earliest recorded interment there was in 1881.

The information had been transcribed by the (W P A) worker from the Carter CRAFFORD Family Bible. The Bible's first owner was Henry CRAFFORD, then William CRAFFORD Sr., William CRAFFORD Jr., and Miss Lucy CRAFFORD, the present owner. This information is recorded here because some of these persons must have been buried at Mulberry Island.

"The first Bible is very old. It is large size and quite thick. The pages are heavy quality of paper which is brown and yellow with age. Some pages are ragged and falling out. The print is Old English. The backs are made of stiff brown material. It was printed in London by Mark BASKET, in the year MDCCLXVII (1767).

The second Bible, the Carter CRAFFORD Family Bible is the large size, and is very thick and heavy. It contains the Old and New Testaments, With Canne's Marriagal References, with Concordance, Index, A Table of Texts, and account of the Lives of the Apostles and Evangelists with pictures. This Bible was published by Robinson and Franklin, New York, in the year 1839.

FIRST BIBLE:
Marriages;
Carter CRAFFORD and Sarah, his wife were married Sunday, May 25, 1777.
Carter CRAFFORD and Martha, his wife were Married Dec. 31, 1789.
John CRAFFORD and Martha C. LANGTHORNE were married Feb. 25, 1802. Thursday eve.
Charles MOORE and Martha CRAFFORD, widow of Charles CRAFFORD, were married April 27, 1800. Sunday evening.
Carter CRAFFORD Jr. and Sarah K. MARROW were married Dec. 11, 1823
Richard C. WYNNE and Sarah A. CRAFFORD, daughter of Henry CRAFFORD and Mary A. S. his wife, were married May 16, 1840.
Wm. C. CRAFFORD and Mary E. F. WALLER were married Feb. 19, 18xx (cannot read).
Wm. C. CRAFFORD and Sarah E. JONES were married Aug. 20, 1848.
Wm. CRAFFORD and Lucy A. CRAFFORD were married Sept 5, 1866.

Births;

John CRAFFORD, son of Carter and Sarah, his wife, was born Saturday nine o'clock in the evening, Dec. 11, 1779.

Elizabeth Gray CRAFFORD was born Saturday May 8, 1874.

Henry CRAFFORD, son of Carter and Martha CRAFFORD was born Monday 10 o'clock in the evening, March 25, 1792.

Carter CRAFFORD, son of Carter CRAFFORD and Martha, his wife, was born Thursday 12 o'clock, April 4, 1799.

Mary Ann CRAFFORD, daughter of Carter and Martha CRAFFORD, was born Friday 11 o'clock in the evening, Dec. 3. 1800.

John Filmer MOORE, son of Carter and Martha CRAFFORD, was born Sunday evening Sept. 24, 1809.

Sarah Elizabeth, daughter of Carter CRAFFORD, was born July 14, 1835.

William Henry CRAFFORD, son of Carter and Sarah, his wife, was born Thursday evening, Sept. 4, 1823.

Sarah Wynne, daughter of Richard C. WYNNE and Sarah, his wife, was born April 25, 1841.

Henry Camm CRAFFORD, son of William CRAFFORD and Mary, his wife, was born Oct. 7, 1840.

Edmund Carter CRAFFORD, son of William CRAFFORD and Mary, his wife, was born June 21, 1847.

William CRAFFORD, son of Wm. C. CRAFFORD and Mary E., his wife, was born May 14, 1845.

John CRAFFORD, son of Wm. C. CRAFFORD and Sarah E., his wife, was born June 24, 1849.

Alice CRAFFORD, daughter of Wm. C. CRAFFORD and Sarah, his wife, was born July 25, 1850.

Charles CRAFFORD, son of Wm. C. and Sarah CRAFFORD was born June 15, 1851.

Emma CRAFFORD, daughter of Wm. C. and Sarah CRAFFORD was born Oct. 7, 1853.

William Carter CRAFFORD, son of Henry CRAFFORD and Mary A. S., his wife, was born Jan. 24, 1817, Tuesday, A. M.

Martha Adderline Milnar CRAFFORD, daughter of Henry CRAFFORD and Mary A. S., his wife, was born Aug. 28, 1818. Friday morn.

Sarah Ann CRAFFORD, daughter of Henry CRAFFORD and Mary A. S. his wife, was born April 19, 1820. Friday morning.

John Henry CRAFFORD, son of Henry CRAFFORD and Mary A. S. his wife, was born Feb. 6, 1822. Wednesday evening.

Mary Ann Shields CRAFFORD, daughter of Henry CRAFFORD and his wife, Mary A., was born Feb. 5, 1824.

Deaths;

Mary Adderline Shield CRAFFORD, wife of Henry CRAFFORD, departed this life March 14, 1824. Sunday Morning 9:10 o'clock, Aged 26 years and 7 days.

Henry CRAFFORD departed this life April 18, 1824. Sunday morning, 42 minutes after 5 o'clock. Aged 33 years and 23 days. His body was committed to earth April 19, 1825.

Martha Adderline Milnar CRAFFORD departed this life July 15, 1825. Friday evening at 4 o'clock. Aged six years, 10 months.

Mary Ann Shields CRAFFORD departed this life Jan 8, 1826. Aged one year and eleven months.

Sarah CRAFFORD, wife of Carter CRAFFORD, departed this life Jan. 1786. Friday, 3 o'clock in the evening.

Carter CRAFFORD departed this life Nov. 10, 1800. Monday nine o'clock in the morning.

Mary Ann CRAFFORD, daughter of Carter CRAFFORD and Martha, his wife, departed this life March 29, 1823, 10:30 A. M. in her twentieth year.

John Filmer MOORE, son of Charles Moore and Martha, his wife, departed this life Sept 18, 1817.

William MARRIETT, son of Matthias and Elizabeth departed this life Nov. 22, 1780.

Elizabeth Gray CRAFFORD, departed this life Oct. 16, 1787.

Charles CRAFFORD departed this life Nov. 10, 1800.

Sarah K. CRAFFORD, wife of Carter CRAFFORD, departed this life the 17th, --- 1839. Sunday morning.

John Henry CRAFFORD, son of Henry CRAFFORD and Mary, his wife, departed this life July 17, 1833. Sunday morning. Age 19 years.

Sarah A. WYNNE, daughter of Henry and Mary CRAFFORD, departed this life May 18, 1841. Age 21 years and 1 month.

Henry Camm CRAFFORD, son of Wm. C. CRAFFORD and Mary E., his wife, departed this life Aug 27, 1845. Age 5yrs, 10mos and 10das.

Mary E. CRAFFORD, wife of Wm. C. CRAFFORD, and daughter of Edmund and Mary Ann WALLER departed this life Oct. 31, 1840.

Carter CRAFFORD, son of Carter and Martha CRAFFORD departed this life Feb. 5, 1849. Age 49 years, 10 months.

Alice CRAFFORD, daughter of Wm. C. and Sarah E. CRAFFORD, departed this life June 26, 1852. Age 1 year, 11 months.

William C. CRAFFORD, son of Henry CRAFFORD and Mary A. S., his wife, departed this life Feb. 5, 1863. Age 46 years, 11 days.

Sarah Fannie CRAFFORD, daughter of William CRAFFORD and Lucy A., his wife, departed this life, Sunday, Feb. 27, 1881. Age 4 yes.

Mildred Alice CRAFFORD, daughter of William CRAFFORD and Lucie A., his wife, departed this life Sunday, April 17, 1881, Age 2 years, 1 month and 18 days.

Virginia Adora CRAFFORD, daughter of William CRAFFORD and Lucie A., his wife, departed this life Thursday, April 21, 1881. Age 1 year, 1 month and 12 days."

A record of 60 African-American slave births are listed dating from 1744 to 1774 with only the first name and birth date given. Anyone researching their African-American ancestry on the Crafford plantation this will find this is a valuable source.

CRAFFORD FAMILY SLAVES CEMETERY
(42) {E 11}

"This cemetery is located 60 yards from the Mulberry Island Road on the present golf course and near the Carter CRAFFORD family plot. There are approximately 50 unidentified African-American graves. This cemetery was probably established before the Civil War for the burial of CRAFFORD family slaves and was continued in use by their descendants. No headstones or markers have been found to identify individuals buried." All vestiges of this cemetery, as well as of the CURTIS and CRAFFORD cemeteries are gone, destroyed in the construction of the golf course 1954-1956.

CRAFFORD FAMILY CEMETERY, FORT CRAFFORD
(44) {A 9}

"This grave site is located about 50 yards east of the house foundation in the center of Fort CRAFFORD. There were never any tombstones at this site, according to a statement made in 1937 by Miss Lucy CRAFFORD, a life long resident of Mulberry Island. These graves were marked by trees planted at each end of the graves. Those graves were not destroyed by the construction of a large artillery battery located there during the Civil War. They are over grown by honeysuckle, underbrush and trees. It is quite likely that any members of the Fort CRAFFORD garrison who died in 1861 - 1862 may also have been buried in or near this plot."

CRAFFORD FAMILY SLAVE CEM., FORT CRAFFORD
(45) {A 10}

"Like the family graves, the number and exact location of the graves is not known. The grave site was located about 100 yards southeast of the family plot, and none of the graves were covered by construction of the Fort CRAFFORD battery. There are records of the births and deaths of some of the slaves in the old CRAFFORD family Bible." (There are mostly births in the Bible).

CURTIS FAMILY CEMETERY
(41) {E 12}

"The Curtis family site was situated on the present golf course near the fir tree about 480 feet east of the Mulberry Island Road. It contains 19 graves. Only six of these were members of the Curtis family, so it presumably took its name from the landowner. This site was the burial place of Dr. H. H. CURTIS, who was the largest landowner on Mulberry Island at the time of the War Between the States. He also organized and commanded the Warwick Beauregards, an infantry company from Warwick County. Dr. CURTIS was the father of Simon CURTIS, who was long active politically in Warwick Country and county treasurer from 1900 to 1944. Other graves in the plot include nine members of the MINER family (MINER family headstones were moved to Lebanon Church of Christ Cemetery), two of the WRIGHT family, one of the WELLS family, and one of the SMITH family, all probably related by marriage.

Sacred
To the Memory of
Dr. H. H. CURTIS
Born
Sept. 6, 1832
Died
Oct. 28, 1881
An Honest man
The Noblest work of God.

Annie Curtis SMITH
Beloved wife of
George Levin SMITH
Born Aug. 8, 1859
Died March 23, 1901

Like some lonely flower that disperses its perfume
And makes our lives happier, so this devoted wife
Affectionate daughter and sister made love and
Joy in the home by her loving deeds, genial
Smiles and cheerful disposition.
Sadly do we miss her but in amid the gloom
That surrounds our aching hearts and falling
Tears, The Star of hope beams brightly, pointing
Where pain and parting all are over
And life is lost in love."

DOZIER ROAD CEMETERY
(12) {I 8}

The following from the Historical Series 4.2A, Nov. 92. Ft. *Eustis Historical & Archaeological Association.*

This site may have been the site of a Colonial Church. This is supported in the contention that this church was also referred to as "The Mulberry Island Chapel". One of the main users was a Methodist group which stopped holding services there when they moved to a new church on Hoopes Road and is now called the Warwick Memorial United Methodist church. After they moved, it became an African-American Church.

Rev. Thomas D. WRIGHT, was the first African-American ordained minister of Gospel in Warwick County and first to establish African-American free school in said county, the first to raise a African-American resident lawyer."

There were four stones near the grave, "LAW" "TGW" AND "WCMM".

Nearby is another grave bearing the headstone of Samuel ARMFIELD. Records show that the Armfield family owned the land fronting on the road near the Greyhound Station.

The following is what is left of the Dozier Road Cemetery:

Samuel Lee ARMFIELD, Jr. Nov 19, 1910 Sept. 28, 1980 Beloved Husband & Father Masonic insignia	T. G. W.
	W. C. M. M. Rev. Thomas D. WRIGHT Died Aug 4, 1891 Age 70 years (very long inscription)
L. A. W.	

Rev. Thomas Wright, Dozier Road

Samuel L. Armfield, Jr.

FITCHETT FAMILY BURIAL GROUND
(46) {D 23}

"The FITCHETT family burial ground is situated in the old garden of the "Water View" home, which is located at the extreme end of Mulberry Island. There are some old trees and approximately nine grave sites. None of these graves are marked, or if they were, the headstones have been removed. The graves are now overgrown with underbrush and honeysuckle vines, making the graves difficult to locate."

JONES HOUSE BURIAL GROUND
(43) {D 8}

"The oldest graveyard known to exist on Mulberry Island was located near the Matthew Jones House. The property was owned by Emmett W. MILSTEAD, then acquired by the U. S. Army in 1918. It has changed hands many times over the years; the JONES, GREENS, FITCHETTS, and WEBBS lived there during the 19th century and the graveyard was used by all of these families. During World War 1, this cemetery was destroyed by the construction of the River Road and railroads. There are no records of how many graves were in this cemetery. It is probable that the first burials were in the 17th century."

MULBERRY ISLAND CEMETERY, CLUB
(48) {D 12}

"This one acre plot was located a short distance beyond the CRAFFORD Family Slave Cemetery, a few hundred yards on the opposite side of the road. There is no record of the interments there but it apparently was a privately owned plot in which the families of the members of the club were buried. This is shown on an Army map dated 1919." (Club not given).

NETTLES FAMILY CEMETERY
(47) {E 12}

"This was a large family that owned various plots of land on Mulberry Island. This cemetery was located just east of Mulberry Island Road, adjacent to the test area railroad spur. It has been leveled. There is no information available as to how many graves were at this site or when it was used."

SAXON'S GAOL - possible graves

"A 1923 report filed at Fort Eustis recounts the findings of a group of soldiers on maneuvers at the tip of Mulberry Island. The report stated that when the soldiers began digging in they uncovered skeletal human remains in an advanced state of decomposition. From the location it could be and the reference of shallow graves, this could be a burial site of prisoners who languished in Saxon's Goal. Popular belief is that this served as the debtors prison also."

WORK PROGRESS ADMIN. CEMETERY
WPA and FERA BURIALS
(29) {I 12}

There are two cemeteries located about 150 yards northeast of the tennis courts on Pershing Avenue. Burials were made at these two plots from December 1934 until October 1936, during the period that the Work Progress Administration (W P A) operated a transient indigent workers' camp at Fort Eustis. The first cemetery contains the graves of nine African-Americans, and the second cemetery holds the graves of thirteen white men who died there during the period of W P A occupancy.

In the 1930's when the Federal Emergency Relief Administration (FERA) and Works Progress Administration (W P A) was in operation, some of the persons working under the Ft. Eustis Administration died and were buried at Ft. Eustis.
The following is a listing of those in the cemetery at Ft. Eustis, taken from the Historical Series 4.2A Nov. 1992, Ft. *Eustis Historical and Archaeological Association.*
Listed in Chronological order

Acknowledgment: Gertrude Stead, compiled information. Col. Jean M. Gray, Research paper in Historical Series 4.2A, Nov. 1992, *Ft. Eustis Historical & Archaeological Association.* Also, *Virginia Historical Inventory, (W P A), The Library of Virginia.*

FERA WORKERS

Thomas MOORE, 56, d. Dec 25, 1934, burial 30th. d. Warwick Co. Jail.
William B. HARDING, 59, d. Jan 29, 1935, burial Mar. 10, d. Riverside Hosp.
Edward ANDERSON, 20, d. Jan. 20, 1935, burial Mar. 10.
Edward O. NEIL, d. Mar. 3, 1935, burial Mar. 10. Killed on Hwy 60 in Warwick.
* Lewis TOWNS, 25, d. Mar. 13 (15), 1935, burial 17th.
Phillip KILLEN, 60, d. Mar 17, 1935, burial 22nd.
* James STOKES, 54, d. June 15, 1935, burial 19th.
* Frank DULY, 43, d. July 12, 1935, burial 19th.
Lee JAMES, 25, d. Sept. 23, 1935, burial 29th. Killed by C&O train near Lee Hall.

WPA WORKERS

Joseph NORMAN, 59, d. Dec. 31, 1935, burial Jan. 12.
William E. SIMMONS, 68, d. Jan 3, 1936, burial 12th.
* George J. FINDLEY, 24, d. Jan. 8, 1936, burial 14th.
Robert LADON, 42, d. Jan. 23, 1936, burial Feb. 21.
* William GASKIN, 35, d. Feb. 10, 1936, burial 26th.
James W. ROSE, 29, d. Apr 4, 1936, burial 18th.
Oakey R. REYNOLDS, 49, d. Apr. 21, 1936, burial 26th.
* Lee McCANN, 28, d. May 6, 1936, burial 13th.
Frank J. TOLEY, 54, d. June 17, 1936, burial 23rd. Dropped dead at Fort Eustis.
Clyde TRISSUE, 36, d. June 27, 1936, burial July 2.
* John BENJAMIN, 25, d. July 25, 1936, burial Aug. 12, Drowned at Manteo, N.C.
* John LAMBRIGHT, 24, Sept. 18, 1936, burial Oct. 7, Drowned at Manteo during storm.
* Joe LEA, 32, d. Sept. 18, 1936, burial Oct. 7, Drowned at Manteo during storm.
* Unmarked grave.
* Unmarked grave.

* Negro. Unless otherwise noted, all died at Grace Hospital, Ft. Eustis.

Work Progress Admin. Cemetery

NEWPORT NEWS PRIMITIVE BAPTIST SERVICE CHURCH CEMETERY
WAS KNOWN AS MORRISON EPISCOPAL
GATEWOOD ROAD (1) {J 33}

Robert James GAMBOL
1842 - 1911
Martha E. Amory GAMBOL
1847 - 1918

Fannie M. DAVIS
Beloved Wife of
E. W. JOHNSON
April 14, 1879
Dec. 12, 1914
At Rest

Lewis L. DAVIS
Son of Mary Y. COPELAND
Died
Oct 27, 1898
Aged
18 yrs, 7 mos, & 4Ds.
One precious to our hearts has gone
The voice we loved is stilled.
The place made vacant
in our home
Can never more be filled!

B. W. COPELAND
Dec. 14, 1850
Sep. 5, 1919

Mother
Mollie Davis
COPELAND
Aug. 4, 1855
April 1, 1928
At Rest

Our Son
Wm. Jennings DAVIS
Oct. 4, 1910
Sept. 28, 1927
Death is the gate of life

Owen GRIFFITHS
1901 - 1929

Unmarked Grave

John Lee SYNDER
U.S. Marine
Corps

Pauline A. BECKER
Born
Jan. 28, 1850
Died
Nov. 15, 1907

Fred J. BECKER
Born
May 23, 1846
Died
Feb. 14, 1913
None knew thee but to love thee

Samuel D. WRIGHT
5 Jan. 1912
28 Jul. 1939
At Rest

Carrington F.
WRIGHT
July 22, 1876
Feb. 16, 1952
At Rest

Margaret L.
WRIGHT
March 10, 1878
Oct. 20, 1925
At Rest

The following is from the *Virginia Historical Inventory, (W P A), The Library of Virginia, 1937*

Col. Jos. Hutchinson
HAM
June 6, 1838
April 25, 1912

His wife
Anna Gambol
April 10, 1844
February 17, 1930
HAM

Henrietta G. GAMBOL
wife of
Oliver P. COPELAND
Born
Dec. 26, 1838
Died
Feb. 11, 1904

The following is from the St. Paul's Episcopal Church, 34th, Street Newport News, Va., history of the church.

In 1880 the Rev. John Gravatt of St. John's, Hampton, obtained $550 from the Diocese and the convocation and was given the Rev. Charles J. S. Mayo as an Assistant for work in Warwick Parish. He preached his first sermon in a schoolhouse at Gum Grove, now known as Morrison. Later, as a result of this early work, the Emmanuel Chapel was built. The building with its graveyard can still be seen behind Warwick High School as a small Baptist Church.

Newport News Primitive Baptist Service Church and Cemetery

Robert James Gambol and Martha E. Amory Gambol

Tombstone at Newport News Primitive Baptist Church Cemetery

PENINSULA MEMORIAL PARK

BETWEEN WARWICK BLVD AND NETTLES DRIVE (9) {K 26}

The Peninsula Memorial Park Cemetery is a very large managed cemetery. There are about 12,000 interments in this cemetery. Because it is such a large cemetery it will not be included in this book. Only, the transcriptions appear here that are from the *Virginia Historical Inventory, (WPA), The Library of Virginia*. These tombstone were transcribed in 1937.

INSCRIPTIONS:
    1832 - 1936

OWNER:
    Peninsula Memorial Park Corporation

DESCRIPTION:
    The gentle slopes of the Memorial Park are a solid expanse of perpetual green dotted with beautiful shrubs and flowers, and interspersed with gracefully contoured drives. The park is surrounded by an iron fence covered with white rambling roses. A central monument, "The Tower of Memories" is a beautiful structure.

HISTORICAL SIGNIFICANCE:
    The Park is a most inspiring memorial, dedicated to our departed - a spot where man and nature have blended their skill, where graceful lines, green lawns and artistic shrubbery breathe a benediction of peace and beauty.
    The following are the inscriptions from the tombstones.

MITCHELL
Joseph T. Mitchell
Born Aug. 22, 1864
Died Dec. 29, 1934
At Rest

FENNIMORE
Lucile Fennimore
1866 - 1932

HAUSER
Alfred Jacob Hauser
1839 - 1932

KELLUM
J. J. Kellum
1855 - 1932

DIEHL
Daniel Huggue Diehl
1860 - 1932

BAUMANN
Henry Baumann
1864 - 1932

CORRICK
Oriana Levina Corrick
1864 - 1932

HOLMSTROM
John Holmstrom
1863 - 1932

LONG
Henry Scharck
Long
1832 - 1933

LONG
Katharine Moses
Long
1850 - 1934

HEMMERICH
Leonard Hemmerich
Born in Frankfortmaine
Germany
1857 - 1933

AMORY
Robert F. Amory
1860 - 1933

FARINHOLT
Thomas J. Farinholt
Born in New Kent Co.
1862 - 1933

WILLIAMS
Margaret Belvidere
Williams
Born in Ashland, Ky.
1863 - 1933

SEAY
John B. Seay
Born in Dinwiddie Co.
1854 - 1933

SMITH
Charles Edward
Smith
1865 - 1933

HOPKINS
Thomas Ederfield
Hopkins
1860 - 1934

SWINERTON
John Robinson
Swinerton
1841 - 1934

JACKSON
Guy Allan Jackson
1863 - 1934

DAVIS
William Bernard
1851 - 1934

BRESELMAN
Ella Collie Breselman
1859 - 1934

MILLER
Nathaniel Fleming
Miller
1861 - 1934

MENCH
Sally Mench
1840 - 1924

MENCH
W. F. Mench
1861 - 1934

MENCH
Hudson Mench
1836 - 1916

SHANKLAND
Archie Shankland
Born Griban, Scotland
1860 - 1934

MARKS
Benjamin Taylor
Marks
1849 - 1934

CONNELL
George E. Connell
1858 - 1934

CONNELL
Kate Connell
1859 - 1936

BRENTLEY
Alfred Brentley, Jr.
1863 - 1937

BURTON
Charles Robinson
Burton
1849 - 1935

McCULLACK
Sarah Alice McCullack
1854 - 1935

MURY
Mary Ellen Mury
1866 - 1935

PETERS
W. M. Peters
1866 - 1935

DELABAR
John Mitchell
Delabar
1849 - 1935

GREGORY
James Gregory
Born in Richmond
1861 - 1935

SIMONSON
Clinton Simonson
1858 - 1935

MILLER
Sue E. Miller
1866 - 1935

JACKSON
Andrew Jackson
1861 - 1935

SMITH
R. T. Smith, Sr.
1834 - 1916

SMITH
Jane E. Smith
1832 - 1891

WEITZ
Elizabeth Weitz
1866 - 1936

VERNON
Charles T. Vernon
1861 - 1936

BLACKWOOD
William Blackwood
Nov. 19, 1866
Mar. 9, 1935

KELLUM
John Jesse Kellum
Nov. 14, 1855
June 8, 1911

KELLUM	GRIST
Maggie Kellum	William A. Grist
1864 - 1888	1864 - 1936

The Peninsula Memorial Cemetery is a very large, well maintained managed cemetery. A transcription of all the interments is not within the scope of this book. It would be a book in it self and should be the future work of a peninsula genealogist or historian.

Acknowledgment: Gertrude Stead for the research and Barry Miles for pictures.

Peninsula Memorial Park, Nettles Drive entrance

Peninsula Memorial Park

Old Section

New Section

PROVIDENCE MENNONITE CHURCH

13101 WARWICK BOULEVARD (6) {K 22}

The following inventory is from the Virginia Historical Inventory, (W P A), The Library of Virginia.

David S. YODER
Mar. 29, 1864
Apr. 29, 1936
At Rest
f/s "Father"

Malinda YODER
May 18, 1865
July 13, 1937
At Rest
f/s "Mother"

Melvin J. YODER
June 26, 1893
April 20, 1944

Ella M. YODER
Died April 27, 1890
Aged 10 months
f/s E.M.Y.

Johny D. YODER
Died June 21, 1902
Aged 3 months
f/s J.D.Y.

Menno B. GLICK
Nov. 15, 1863
April 10, 1940

Minnie GLICK
Aug. 28, 1865
Jan. 3, 1948

Hazel GLICK
1894 - 1974

Mother
Mary Elizabeth
BURLESON
Aug. 8, 1889
Mar. 14, 1932

Martha H.
Wife of
Henry SHELLEY
Born May 18, 1875
Died Aug. 12, 1912
*Blessed are the dead that
die in the Lord for though
They are dead yet shall
They live*

Henry SHELLEY
Born Jan. 14, 1880
Died Sept. 4, 1935
*A loved one gone to rest
you will always be
remembered by the
ones that loved you best*

Jacob H.
Son of
Henry & Mary
SHELLEY
Born Oct. 5, 1914
Died Nov. 12, 1924
*Infant son of Henry
& Mary SHELLEY*

Husband
William D.
LANGREHR
April 26, 1852
May 3, 1932

Emily C. MAPES
Born Feb. 18, 1937
Died June 9, 1937

Michael S. BUTCHER
April 11, 1952
April 11, 1952

SMOKER
Wilbur H   Alta M.
1915 - 1972   1913
57y 1m 10d

Father
Christian K. MILLER
Born Dec. 6, 1859
at Maulbrum
Wurtemberg Germany
Died Apr. 19, 1910

Mother
Abbie M. MILLER
March 12, 1849
June 17, 1928
*In that beautiful home
we'll meet each other again*

Abi Virginia
MILLER
Born Nov. 23, 1900
Died
Aug. 3, 1901

Joel ZOOK
Died
May 5, 1915
Aged 76 Years
Rest Thou Loved one

Father
Rev. Joseph ZOOK
Born
May 28, 1845
Died
Oct. 7, 1918

Mother
Sallie ZOOK
Born
Feb 14, 1851
Died
Jan 27, 1928

Abraham
KURTZ
Born
Aug 28, 1854
Died
April 6, 1922

MAST
Emma C.
Nov. 12, 1895
Mar. 13, 1992
Rest in Peace

MAST
John Z.   Lizzie M.
1856 - 1945   1862 - 1948
Peacefully Sleeping

Rebecca Edna
MAST
Nov. 18, 1897
June 7, 1900

Sarah Leta
MAST
Jan. 30, 1901
Aug. 11, 1901

Elsie Lucille
MAST
June 8, 1903
Oct. 30, 1903

ZVERCHER
Elliott H.   Edna I.
1908 - 1974   1908

Jonathan Stephen LEE
October 9 - 11, 1973
*And Jesus took the
child up and blessed him*

Baby Boy HARPER
(No Headstone)
Info. from Gloria Butcher

Barbara Lee
HARPER
April 11, 1983

BRUBAKER
Adin   Hulda S.
Oct. 28, 1902   Jan. 7, 1907
                 Mar 19, 1982

SUMMERFIELD
Delton   Fay L.
1919 - 1981   1922 -

Acknowledgment: The following is from, Mr. Hutchison's Boy Scout Troop # 108 and Gertrude Stead for her research and photographs.

GLICK
Samuel H.   Lydia S.
Oct. 12, 1862   Aug. 10, 1863
May 17, 1920   Ma6 22, 1944
foot stones

Emery E. GLICK
July 27, 1889
Feb. 9, 1980

Clara GLICK
Oct. 17, 1878
Dec. 14, 1960

Brother
John G. GLICK
Feb. 23, 1896
Nov. 14, 1980

Beulah S. GLICK
Jan. 1, 1894
Jan. 3, 1986

Archie GRAMMAR
1883 - 1961

John HOUSE
Dec. 17, 1901   Jan. 5 , 1962

Carl E. HART, Jr.
April 8, 1962
Nov. 8, 1962

HOSTETTER
Father   Mother
Alpheus M.   Kathryn S.
1883 - 1968   1885 - 1977

Donald LESTLT
1945 - 1977
Andrew - Faulkner

Izetta B. YODER
Jan. 3, 1893
Aug. 7, 1990

Clarence P. YODER
Sept. 24, 1896
Nov. 9, 1983

Elizabeth B. YODER
April 4, 1911
March 5, 1943

Loran J. SMUCKER
Nov. 20, 1913
May 3, 1914

Husband
Clyde F. EMSWILDER
1913 - 1937

Father
Wm. S. LONGAGHER
Sept. 6, 1868
Nov. 18, 1938

Mother
Mary LONGAGHER
June 10, 1880
Oct. 8, 1948

J. R.
MILLER
1871 - 1949

Mother
Magdalena
MILLER
Mar. 17, 1873
Sept. 5, 1942

Providence Mennonite Church Chapel

Providence Mennonite Church and Cemetery

WARWICK MEMORIAL CEMETERY

40 HOOPES ROAD (23) {L 17}

Warwick Memorial Cemetery was located in back of a cinder block building next to the Warwick Memorial United Methodist Church. These graves have been moved to Peninsula Memorial Cemetery, Warwick Boulevard.

Acknowledgment: Gertrude Stead for transcriptions and photographs.

Ralph Arnold	Carrie Norton
SHENE	SHENE
Jan 2, 1873	June 23, 1866
no date	July 21, 1928

On what bright immortal shore
we meet no more to part

John Toomer GARROW
September 25, 1879
November 27, 1938

From *Virginia Historical Inventory (W P A), The Library of Virginia.*

James T. GARROW
1849 - 1929

Robert T. HOLLOWAY
March 7, 1861
Aug. 1, 1929

Carnelia N. W. GARROW
1860 - 1922

Warwick Memorial Cemetery

WARWICK RIVER MENNONITE CHURCH CEMETERY

LUCAS CREEK ROAD (7) {G 19}

The Warwick River Mennonite Church would not allow the tombstones to be transcribed on the 2nd of June 1995. The Tidewater Genealogical has hereby abided by this request.

Acknowledgment: Research and Photographs, Gertrude Stead

The following is from the *Virginia Historical Inventory (W P A), The Library of Virginia*.

Owners:
Warwick River Mennonite Church
Description:
The Mennonite graveyard is located on the sloping side of a small ravine, extending into an open field. There are several large oak trees in the cemetery. This graveyard is quite large. It is kept in excellent condition.

The following inscriptions were copied from tombstones:

Father
Jacob W.
KRAUS
Aug. 1, 1844
June 20, 1915
d/s w/Elizabeth A.

Mother
Elizabeth A.
KRAUS
Jan. 23, 1849
Nov. 30, 1925
d/s w/ Jacob W.

Mother
Anna BRENNEMAN
born
Oct. 7, 1858
Died
Jan. 5, 1934
Aged 75 yrs.

Father
Benjamin BRENNEMAN
Born
Sept. 27, 1855
Died
Feb. 8, 1919
Aged 63 yrs.

Grandfather
John
KEMPF
Mar. 18, 1816
Nov. 6, 1904

William L.
WOODLAND
Born
May 28, 1826
Died
April 28, 1911

Mother
Fannie V. SHENK
Born
Oct. 30, 1865
Died
Oct. 3, 1904
Earth has no sorrow
that Heaven cannot heal

Simon P. YODER
1847 - 1926
O Glorious Thought
from Death to rise
and be forever
with the Lord

Jacob HAHN
1839 - 1926

In Memory of
Martin B. SHENK
Sept. 7, 1854
Mar. 6, 1930
d/s w/ Catharine

Joseph HERTZLER
Jan. 7. 1849
May 13, 1920

Nancy J. MILLER
his wife
Mar. 3, 1857
Jan 19, 1915

Fannie
Wife of I. D. HERTZLER
Born Aug. 14, 1855
Died Oct. 15, 1910
Aged 55 years
A loved one from us has gone
A voice we love is stilled
A place is vacant in our Home
Which never can be filled

Anna HAHN
1849 - 1933

In Memory of
Catharine SHENK
Oct. 31, 1852
Aug. 12, 1912
d/s w/Martin B.

Warwick River Mennonite Church Cemetery

WILBERN GRAVEYARD

BLUNT POINT ROAD (33) {E 28}

The information on this cemetery is from the *Virginia Historical Inventory (W P A), The Library of Virginia*, the *William and Mary Quarterly, Volumes 14 and 15, Series 1*, 1905 - 1907, and Parks Rouse's book, "*Endless Harbor*".

From the Virginia Historical Inventory; 1937

Location:
7.2 miles south of Denbigh, Virginia, on route #60, thence 1.6 miles west on Route #100, thence 0.3 of a mile south on private road, on east side.

Date:
1741, date of oldest grave.

Owner:
Roscow family were the original owners.
Wilbern family are the present owners.

This graveyard originally belonged to the Roscow estate, and was called the Roscow burying ground. In later years the Wilberns bought the property, and some of the family were buried there. Now it is called the Wilbern burying ground.

Description:
This family burying ground lies not far distant from the site of the colonial house in a field, but a small group of tall trees guard the sacred ground and turn away the ploughshares. A single tomb remains on the plot, and that has been remodelled in recent years. A new brick base was made, and the broken slab was cemented together. The inscriptions are barely readable. Above the inscriptions there appears the coat of arms, a lion rampant, surrounded by a helmet and scroll work. There is evidence of other graves, but there are no markers. This graveyard is not kept in good condition.

Historical significance:
Here was the last resting place of one of the most illustrious descendants of the Roscow family, William Roscow, and his wife, Mary Wilson. Through the interest of Miss Elizabeth Ivy, this old tomb has been preserved in recent years. The old burying ground is still used. A number of the Wilbern family, who now own the tract, were buried there as late as 1922. Other graves of more recent years are those of an old Negro house servant, formerly a slave in the Wilbern family, and an old hermit who lived in a shack on the place, and was found dead about twenty five years ago on his doorstep. He was given a last resting place beside the scions of the Roscow and Wilbern families.

Following is the inscription from the Roscow tomb;

Under this stone lyeth the Body of William ROSCOW Gentle-
man who was born at Charley in the County of Lancaster on
the 30th day of
November Anno dom 1661
And departed this life at Blunt Point in Ye County of
Warwick the X day of
November Anno dom 1705
And in the 36th year of his age
Also here lies the Body of Mary wife
of above William ROSCOW
And Daughter of Col. Wm. WILSON
of Elizabeth City County who
Was born in Oct. 1675
and dyed Jan. the 11, 1741, in the
67th year of her age.

Source of information:
Tombstone Inscriptions.
"*Foundations Bear Mute Evidence of Former Grandeur*", and article in the *Daily Press* of Newport News, Virginia, page 12, published Sunday, November 18, 1928.

From the *William and Mary Quarterly*:

The tombstone inscription is given same as above, with the following exceptions: "County of Warwick the X day of November Anno dom 1700".

From Parke Rouse's "*Endless Harbor*" on page 8 is a picture of the tomb, and the following quote " The lonely grave of William Roscow, Gentleman, is located in the woods at Blunt Point. It is said to be Virginia's oldest marker". Picture of tomb shows signs of vandalism.

Acknowledgment: Gertrude Stead for her research.

YOUNG FAMILY CEMETERY

WEST GOVERNOR DRIVE (24) {F 23}

The land located at the mouth of the Warwick River and Deep Creek in 1690 was called Warwicktown. The town site was purchased by Richard Young in December 1813. Young petitioned the General Assembly for Denbigh Plantation. By 1813 Richard Young owned the entire Denbigh Plantation and operated the water mill. The water mill, "Young's Mill," was moved to Warwick Boulevard and is on the Newport News Historical Register.

The Young Family Cemetery is located on W. Governor Road in back of the Hunt property. There is an easement across the Hunt's property, but you have to ask permission to cross. The Cemetery is still owned by the Young Family. It is not a large area, with only nine tombstones, but may have unmarked graves. It is surrounded by a wrought iron fence with ground ivy growing over the graves and is well shaded. Some years ago tombstones were stolen, but were replaced with new ones. Hence in the WPA report Ann Benson Green's tombstone read "A good woman" but her new tombstone has "She was a good Woman". The cemetery has nine headstones and two foot stones.

Acknowledgment: Gertrude Stead for research, transcribing and photographs.

The book "*Newport News, 1607-1960*" by Annie Lash Jester, Published by the City of Newport News, Virginia, 1961.

Virginia Historical Inventory (W P A), The Library of Virginia.

L. B. Weber, Newport News, Va.

The following is from the above sources; information in {} is from the WPA records.

John Alden GREEN
1842 - 1873

Double Stone
Durog Hughes JONES
February 21, 1842
July 15, 1896
Mary Green
His wife
August 2, 1844
March 22, 1927

(foot stone D H J)

W. H. LINLEY-KENT
Aug. 22, 1873
Jan 23, 1931
Peace

William G. {Garrow} YOUNG
Born March 21, 1814
Died March 26, 1893
at Denbigh, Va.

Elizabeth Mc Mcoy YOUNG
Daughter of Wm. & Ann Green Young
Born Denbigh Plantation
Sept 9, 1872 - Died Feb 11, 1948
Make to be number with the saint the
saint in glory

Mary Hughs JONES
1878 - 1878

Ann Warwick YOUNG
Wife of
William Henry LINLEY-KENT
Died Sept 3, 198
memory is only friend grievance
can call her own

Anne B. {Benson} YOUNG
{wife of
William G. YOUNG}
Born June 18, 1832
Died April 3, 1893
at Denbigh, Va.
She was a good woman
{A good Woman}

George B. YOUNG
son of
William and
Ann Green YOUNG
Sept 1, 1805
Nov 25, 1961

Foot stone
M. G. J.(Mary Green JONES)

Young Family Cemetery

    M J 63
    Major L. 63
    W H 63

ALLEN
    Edward 44, 57
    Rosa L. 4

ALLMOND 6
    George W. 11

ALLRED
    James Mercer 62

ALTWEGG
    Genevieve Bonewell 56
    Robert Emil 56

AMORY
    Robert F. 119

ANDERSON
    Edward 113

ARMFIELD
    Samuel Lee 109

ARRINGTON
    William H. 9

ASKEW
    John I. 93
    Susie M. 93

BAILEY
    Crayer 3
    Sam 3

BAINES
    John Alfronza 96
    S. Joseph 96
    Zelia Ann 96

BAKER
    Edward M. 9
    Henrietta G. M. 9
    Mary L. 9
    Nelson 9
    William M. 9

BANK
    Arlene 8

BANKS
    L. J. 10
    Moses Lester 7
    Thomas 2

BARRANT
    Icah G. 9
    Icah Keith 10

BAUMANN
    Henry Baumann 118

BAY-TOP
    James 18
    Sarah E. S. 18

BECKER
    Fred J. 115
    Pauline A. 115

BEER
    John C. 71
    Lisetta 71

BENJAMIN
    John 113

BERRY
    Cleveland L. 93
    Clevland L. 93

BERTHA
    Emma D. 11
    J. 11

BEVERIDGE
    Joseph E. 1

BISHOP
    E B 62
    F J 62
    Walter Lee 62

BLACK
    J. H. 6
    John E. 2
    Susian 11
    William T. 62
    Wm. J. 62

BLACKWOOD
    William 120

BLAND
    Theodore M. 9

BLEWFORD
    Lawrence 2

BLOOK?
    Gladys 6

BLUEFORD
    John 7
    Lawrence 6

BONEWELL
    Ann 46
    Charles 57
    Grady R. 57
    James F. 57
    Sarah E. 57
    Wm. J. 46

BOOKER
    Rosanna J. 4

BOOTH
    A T 4

BOYD
    Daisy M. 5
    James L. 4

BOYKIN
    Frederick A. 6

BOZARD
    Earl H. 52

BRENNEMAN
    Anna 130
    Benjamin 130

BRENTLEY
    Alfred 120

BRESELMAN
    Ella Collie 119

BRIGGS
    Helen W. 9

BROWN
    Bernice W. 1
    Jeanette Esther 9
    Liza 3
    Mary 1

BRUBAKER
    Adin 125
    Hulda S. 125

BRYAN
    Edward Eugene 72
    George Edward 86
    Irodeen Harwood 86
    Richard Miles 72

BURCHER 47
    C. C. 59
    Carl E. 59
    Clifton C. 59
    Nina R. 59
    Virginia B. 59

BURLESON
    Delton 125
    Fay L. 125
    Mary Elizabeth 123

BURN
    Eddie Samuel 72

BURNHAM
    William C. 47

BURTON
    Charles 120

BUTCHER
    Michael S. 124

BUTLER
    Archie 93
    Emily 93

BUTTS
    Hariet Anna 12
    Pattie 12

BYRDSONG
    Eva S. 2

CALLIS
    Alan Keith 72

CAMPBELL
    Claudia Cpelan Varn ... 72
    Hugh A. 72
    Hugh Alexander 72
    Martha Curtis 72

CARY
    Alice 98
    Ann 100
    Annie 11
    Brigette 98
    Columbia 18
    Corinne 4
    Daniel 4
    Elizabeth 98
    Gill A. 18
    Gill Armistead 18
    Henry 98
    Jane 98
    John 98
    John 18
    John B. 18
    Mary 100
    Miles 98, 100
    Suaan 18
    Susannah 18
    Thomas 98
    William 98
    Wilson 100

CEREZO
    Mary 72

CHANDLER
    Fern Llewellyn 61

CHAPMAN
    Joanna 10
    Steven 10

CHARLES
    Addie Gray 72
    Betty Page 72
    E. C. 36
    E. G. 36
    J. Allen 72
    J. Henry 72
    John A. 71
    Lewis P. 36
    Louisa D. 71
    Martha J. 36
    Maud B. 72

    Wm. J. 72
CHENOWETH
    Emma Leake 72
    George Durbin 72
CHEVIONRS
    Thedora M 4
CHILDRESS
    John B. 57
    Lelia A. 57
CHO
    Myong Kum 40
CHRISTIAN
    Annie 5
    J C 2
    Winnie 6
CHUN
    Hyun Ja 40
CLARKE
    Ashton W. 72
    Nannie Read 73
CLEMENTS
    Jacob H. 71
    Thomas F. 73
COFER
    Erma 6
    Florence 6
COLE
    Ann 31
    Daughter of William 32
    Digges 31, 32
    Edward 32
    Edward 31
    John 31, 32
    Martha 31
    Mary 31, 32
    Wife of William 32
    William 32
    William 31, 32
COLEMAN
    Estherine 5
    Leroy 5
COMBS
    Ernest 10
    Helen T. 10
    Henry Lee 7
    Rechetta 9
    Rosetta B. 7
CONNELL
    George E. 120
    Kate 120
COOKE
    Alice Minson 73
    Alice Nelson 83
    Dorothy Saxby 73
    K L 59
    Lula Vernella 59
    P E 59
    Philip Roscoe 59
    S. Minson 73
    Stafford G. 73
COPELAND
    B. W. 115
    Mary A. C. 66
    Mary F. 43, 64
    Mary Y. 115
    Mollie Davis 115
    Oliver P. 116
COPELLAN

    Rebecca 7
CORRICK
    Oriana Levina 118
CRAFFORD
    Alice 105, 106
    Andrew C. 73
    Annie C. 74
    Carter 104-106
    Carter 73, 74, 79
    Charles 104-106
    Edmund Carter 105
    Edward T. 73
    Elizabeth Gray 105, 106
    Emma 105
    Emma V. 74
    Eva Salter 73
    Helen M. 73
    Henry 104-106
    Henry 106
    Henry Camm 105, 106
    Henry V. 74
    Infant 73, 74
    John 105
    John 73
    John C. 73
    John E. 73
    John Filmer 105
    John Henry 105, 106
    Lucie A. 106
    Lucy 104
    Lucy 74, 79
    Lucy A. 74, 104, 106
    Lucy Harwood 74
    Lucy L. 73
    M. Alice 74
    M. Josiphine 73
    M. V. 73
    Martha 104-106
    Martha Adderline Milh 105, 106
    Mary 105, 106
    Mary 80
    Mary A. S. 105, 106
    Mary Adderline Shield . 105
    Mary Ann 105, 106
    Mary Ann Shields . 105, 106
    Mary E. 105, 106
    Mary Waller 73
    Mildred Alice 106
    Sarah 104-106
    Sarah A. 104
    Sarah Ann 105
    Sarah E. 74, 106
    Sarah Elizabeth 105
    Sarah Fannie 106
    Sarah K. 106
    Sarah Wynne 105
    V. Adora 74
    Virginia Adora 106
    William 104-106
    William C. 74, 106
    William Carter 105
    William Henry 105
    Wm. 73, 74
    Wm. C. 73, 104-106
CURTIS
    ----- 70
    A. C. 39
    Ann 36

    Ann E. 37
    Ann G. 37
    Anna E. 39
    Annie G. 39
    Annie Sims 74
    Arthur 63
    B. G. 36
    Carter Coleman 74
    Charles 38, 39
    Charley W. 38
    Christopher C. 74
    Corinne B. 74
    D. P. 36
    Daughter of 39, 70
    Douglas Cary 74, 75
    Dr. H. H. 108
    Edith Pitts 74
    Elizabeth G. 37
    Elizabeth Read 75
    Emma Chewning 75
    Fannie S. 38
    Frances Cary 75
    Frank Lee 60
    Georgie Haughton 63
    H. V. 39
    Hortense 38
    John E. 39
    John L. 37
    John L. 38
    John Y. 39
    Lizzie 38
    Lizzie Gibb 38
    Lloyd E. 75
    Lloyd Elton 75
    Lucie F. 38
    Margaret 39
    Maria E. Whitaker 75
    Martha Harwood 36
    Mary Ann 66
    Mary E. 38, 39
    Mary Lee 75
    Miles C. 38
    Minnie F. Shawver 75
    Murcer 38
    Nannie L. Cooke 75
    Nevada B. 75
    Pearlia 39
    R. T. 70
    Robert 37, 38
    Robert C. 38
    Robert Grigs 37
    Robert Thomas 75
    Sam'l G. 36
    Simon C. 75
    Simon Reid 75
    T. C. 37
    T. Gibbs 39
    Thos. 36
    V. C. 38
    W. D. 39
    W. H. 36
    William Oliver 38
DABNEY
    Barney 11
    Lavina 2
    Pastor C. 2
    Walker 6
DAMAN

	C. M. 75	
	L. S. 75	
	Ralph Edwards 75	
DAVIS		
	Alice A. 57	
	Allen 89	
	Allen 90	
	Angie 90	
	Angie L. 89	
	Blanche 56	
	Catherine W. 2	
	Edward H. 63	
	Ethel B. 56	
	Fannie M. 115	
	Frances L. 89	
	George A. 3	
	Hazel Priece 89	
	James G. 57	
	John L. 56	
	Lewis L. 115	
	Mary 3	
	R. Lee 89, 90	
	Richard L. 89	
	Robert Lewis 89	
	Sarah 89	
	Sarah E. 89, 90	
	Senie Moss 56	
	Stanley 8	
	Vernon Elmore 56	
	W. G. 89	
	William Bernard 119	
	William H. 57, 90	
	Wm. Jennings 115	
De VIGNIER		
	Helen Harwood 75	
	Joaquin Robert 75	
DeBERRY		
	Jeanette K. 52	
	Lenmere L. 52	
	Lorraine F. 52	
	Mark S. 52	
	Mark Wayne 52	
DELABAR		
	John 120	
DIEHL		
	Daniel Huggue 118	
DIGGES		
	Cole 45, 48	
	Dudley 31	
	Edward 31	
DIGGIS		
	Alice Ida 8	
	Edward 10	
	Seldon 8	
DIGGS		
	Maggie 6	
	Mary L. 7	
	Susan 6	
	Viola E. 5	
	Virginia T. 8	
DODSON		
	Editha 7	
DODWON		
	James Andrew 1	
DOLAN		
	Margaret D. 46	
	Samuel F. 46	
DONNELLY		
	Elizabeth Parker 62	
DOUGLAS		
	Robert C. 8	
DUFFEY		
	Kenneth E. 40	
DULY		
	Frank 113	
DUNN		
	John 75	
	Lulie Harwood 75	
EALEY		
	Reubven 5	
EDLOW		
	Eva L. 5	
	Virgie 9	
EDWARDS		
	Clara D. 3	
	Custis 3	
ELEY		
	Wilhemina 6	
ELROD		
	Perry W. 55	
EMSWILDER		
	Clyde F. 126	
ENOS		
	Mildred Hogge 62	
	William Warner 62	
EPPERSON		
	Preston T. 75	
	Robert Coleman 76	
	Ruby Steele 76	
EVERSICH		
	Susie Smith 49	
FARINHOLT		
	Thomas J. 119	
FENNIMORE		
	Lucile 118	
FERNANDES		
	Ann 9	
FIELDS		
	Albert 12	
FINDLEY		
	George J. 113	
FITCHETT		
	Lillian 84	
FLEMING		
	Martha Fannie 76	
	T. H. 76	
	Thomas Hayes 76	
FLETCHER		
	Annal 76	
	E. C. 76	
	Infant 76	
	J. W. 76	
	Janet Rae 76	
	Pircy C. 76	
	Robert M. 76	
	Robert Murcher 76	
FOWLER		
	W. Lacy 54	
FOX		
	_____ 6	
	Ambridge 6	
	Anna E. 53	
	Benjamin C. 60	
	Benjamin C. 53	
	Charlie C. 60	
	Delbert C. 53	
	Estelle Cary 5	
	Etta F. 53	
	G. L. 53	
	George Leroy 53	
	Jefferson A. 6	
	Mary C. 76	
	Milton F. 60	
	Robert E. 5	
	Sarah Frances 53	
	Viola Sreves 53	
FOX-CORBITT		
	Thelma G. 61	
FRANCIS		
	Douglas 7	
	Earnest 4	
	Fernando 10	
	Lillian W. 7	
FRANKLIN		
	Thomas 62	
GALLATIN		
	Samuel D. Y. 93	
GAMBOL		
	Henrietta G. 116	
	James T. 66	
	John 66	
	Marhta J. 66	
	Martha E. Amory 115	
	Mary E. 66	
	Robert James 115	
	William 66	
GARRETT		
	Elvira Cavileer 46	
	Eugene Jackson 46	
	Ida Estelle 46	
	Lila M. 59	
GARROW		
	Ann C. 39	
	Ann D. 37	
	Carnelia N. W. 128	
	Cornelia 39	
	James T. 128	
	John 39	
	John L 37	
	John T. 37	
	John Toomer 128	
	Martha A. 37	
	Martha T. 37	
	Samuel 39	
	Thos. J. 37	
	Virginia Curtis 37	
	William H. 37	
GASKIN		
	William 113	
GAYLE		
	Naomi A. 6	
GEORGE		
	Anthony 62	
GIBSON		
	Joan Ann 64	
	M. A. 64	
	R. H. 64	
GILMAN		
	Marylou B. 55	
GLICK		
	Beulah S. 125	
	Clara 125	
	Emery E. 125	
	Hazel 123	

  John G. 125
  Lydia S. 125
  Menno B. 123
  Minnie 123
  Samuel H. 125
GODSEY
  N. M. 57
GOULD
  Dorothea T. 76
  Kenneth M. 76
GRAMMER
  Archie 125
GRAY
  Carrie 9
  Clifton 9
GREEN
  Bennett Wood 43, 55
  John Alden 135
GREGORY
  James 120
GRIFFIN
  David Mercer 62
GRIFFITHS
  Owen 115
GRIST
  William A. 121
GROOM
  Samuel Seldner 14
HABBELL
  Sam'l H. 80
  Sarah Langley 80
HAHN
  Anna 131
  Jacob 131
HAHNN
  Virginia 94
HALL
  Annie Virginia 47
  Sarah E. 47
  William B. 47
HAM
  Anna Gambol 116
  Jos. Hutchinson 116
HARDING
  William B. 113
HARPER
  Baby Boy 125
  Barbara Lee 125
HARRIS
  Annie E. 52
  Annie O. 53
  Annie O. 63
  Catharine 53
  Children 53
  Infant Dan 53
  Jennette 53
  Mammie C. 2
  Martha I. 52
  Mildred H. 52
  R. M. 53
  Richard T. 52
  Robert M. 63
  William 2
  Willie A. 52
HARRISON
  Benjamin 45
  Diggs 45
  Elizabeth 45
  Mary 45, 48
  Nathaniel 45
  Nathaniel 48
HART
  Carl E. 125
HARWOOD
  Alexander Gilliam 76
  D. G. H. 69
  E. C. 77
  E. M. 69
  Elizabeth 80
  George Montgomery 76
  George Washington 76
  H. K. 69
  Indiana Virginia 77
  John L. 69
  L. G. 77
  L. M. T. 69
  N. L. 69
  Wm. 80
HAUGHTON
  Annie C. 60
  Armistead 63
  Armstead 43
  Charlotte W. 63
  R. E. 60
  William Armistead 59
  Woodrow Wilson 60
HAUSER
  Alfred Jacob 118
HAWLEY
  James H. T. 50
  Laura B. 51
  Paul E. 50
  Sallie A. 50
  William S. 50
  Wm. S. 51
HAYES
  Olive Fox 60
  Willis 5
HEMMERICH
  Leonard 119
HERBERT
  Robert B. 2
HERTIZLER
  Fannie 131
HERTZLER
  Joseph 131
HEYWOOD
  Audrey V. 63
  Homer L. F. 64
  W. T. 64
  Walter Thomas 64
  Wm. Morris 64
HOBSON
  Henry 98
HOGGE
  Daisy 62
  Irene Lee 60
  Laura M. 77
  Norrie Lee 61
  Thomas Franklin Jr 62
  Thomas Joseph 60
  W. A. Sammy 77
  William Everette 61
  Willie M. 61
  Wilton George 51
HOLLOWAY
  Helen M. 58
  Infant Daughter 58
  M H 58
  Robert H. 58
  Robert T. 128
HOLMES
  Sadie 5
  Willie L. 5
HOLMSTROM
  John 119
HOOD
  Ethel Julia 77
  James Ralph 77
HOOVER
  David A. 40
HOPKINS
  Cora Lukhard 62
  M. T. 89
  Mary F. 58
  Thomas Ederfield 119
HOPSON
  George Dewey 1
  J. M. 1
HORN
  Henry L. 77
  Mary Epperson 77
  Willie J. 77
HORNSBY
  Alice S. 49
  Helen M. 77
  Rebecca 44, 49
  Romelus 49
  William 49
  William 44
HOSTETTER
  Alpheus M. 125
  Infant 47
  Kathryn S. 125
  R. T. 47
HOUGHTON
  Alda S. 61
  Elizabeth 60
  Elizabeth Black 61
  J. Langhorne 60
  Robert 61
HOWARD
  Sarah Elizabeth 57
HUBBARD
  Frances N. 93
  William N. 93
HUDGINS
  Enniel L. 1
  Hanna 3
  John 3
  Saac C. 1
  Solomon 7
  Thomas 1
  Tommie 3
HUDSON
  George 2
  Silas 7
HUGGUNS
  S. 1
HUGHES
  Gracie 5
  William P. 1
HUNDLEY
  Ruth Cary 9

HUNT
- Lauren Davis 56

HURLEY
- Mollie Weymouth 77

HUTCHINS
- Sarah 77
- T. C. 77

JACKSON
- Andrew 120
- Guy Allan 119
- Jane E. 120
- R. T. 120

JAMES
- Lee 113

JARVIS
- Dorothy J. 4
- Frank 4
- Henry 4
- Louise White 4
- Maggie 4
- Samuel L. 10
- W. H. 4

JEFFERSON
- Lena M. 8

JENKINS
- Lueatta C. 1

JENNINGS
- George W. 9

JOHNSON
- E. W. 115
- Elsie Epperson 77
- Flottie Bertha 11
- Floyd Wilmer 77
- Frank E. 64
- Freddie L 4
- Helen J. 64
- Jacob H. 55
- Mary E. 43
- Mary E. 54
- Mattie E. 7
- Sallie F. 55
- William J. 55

JOINS
- Ed. 12
- Fanny 12

JONES
- Bertha E. 5
- D. P. 41
- Dempsey D. 38
- Durog Hughes 135
- Earl D. 7
- J. M. 11
- Lelia Wynn 5
- Magruder B. 64
- Margaret E. 38
- Mary 10
- Mary E. 2
- Mary F. 43
- Mary F. 64
- Mary Green 135, 136
- Mary Hughs 136
- Sam 10
- Sarah E. 104
- William Y. 64
- Wm. A. 77

JORDAN
- Eva M. 77
- Lucy B. 77

JUNG
- Kyu Young 40

JURLINGTON
- Annie R. 44
- Sarah E. 43
- W. H. 43

KAP
- So Sun 40

KELLUM
- Elizabeth 47
- Emma D. 46
- George W. 46
- J. 47
- J. J. 118
- Jesse 47
- John Jesse 120
- Maggie 121
- Marcacel 47

KEMPF
- John 130

KETCHMORE
- Jack H. 9
- Willie 9

KEYES
- Arlethia 7
- Patsey 8

KEYS
- Alma C. 2

KILLEN
- Phillip 113

KIM
- Christiana 40

KIRBY
- Banister P. 78
- Benjamin H. 8
- Calie D. 78
- Cora B. 78
- Earl Lee 78
- Elizabeth 78
- Etta Diggs 8
- Harwood 78
- Irene Curtis 78
- Jack 78
- Josephine Maude 78
- Julia V. 78
- Nellie B. 82
- Vernon W. 78
- William H. 78
- William P. 78

KNAUFF
- Mary Anna Kirby 78

KRAUS
- Elizabeth A. 130
- Jacob W. 130

KURTZ
- Abraham 124

LADON
- Robert 113

LAMBRIGHT
- John 113

LAND
- Mark A. 60

LANGFORD
- Ernest 9
- Jessie R. 9

LANGREHR
- William D. 124

LANGTHORNE
- Martha C. 104

LEA
- Joe 113

LEAR
- John 31, 32

LEE
- A. 90
- E. T. 89
- Edna B. 78
- Frank 79, 81
- Jonathan Stephen 125
- Martha E. 89
- Myrtle E. 79, 81
- R. D. 89
- Robert H. 89
- Wm. 90

LEEBA
- Walter 7

LESTLT
- Donald 126

LEWELLING
- John W. 43, 63

LEWIS
- Bettie Lee 51
- Willie A. 8

LICON
- John Thomas 8
- Roberta S. 8

LINLEY-KENT
- W. H. 135
- William Henry 136

LINWOOD
- S. O. 47
- Henry 47
- W. S. 47

LIPFORD
- Edward 11
- Piant 11

LLEWELLYN
- John A. 61
- Ruby O. 61
- Sarah M. 61

LONG
- Henry Scharck 119
- Katharine Moses 119

LONGAGHER
- Mary 126
- Wm. S. 126

LUERSSEN
- Baby 95
- Frank B. 95
- George 95
- Julia E. 95
- Julia Etta 95

LUSBY
- Lester C. 79

LYLISTON
- Ann Bachelor 94
- Carrie B. 94
- David 95
- Martha Susan 94
- Richard 94
- Richard J. 94
- Thomas David 93, 94
- William Henry Clay ... 94

LYNCH
- Fannie B. 56
- Wilson M. 56

MADISON
- Mary 52
- W. B. 52

MAGILLEY
- Edward J. 46

MALLACHI
- Samuel 2

MALLICOTT
- John M. 64

MALLICOTTE
- George I. 51
- James D. 51
- John E. 51
- Pauline 51
- William H. 51

MANEY
- Alice R. 93
- Allie G. 96
- Ann P. 96
- Burckett 95
- Clara 96
- Clara L. 97
- Mallory 93
- Roland L. 96
- S. R. 96
- Stephen 96
- Stephen R. Hayes .. 96
- Stephen R. Hayes .. 96
- Thomas L. 95

MAPES
- Emily C. 124

MARKS
- Benjamin Taylor ... 120

MARRIETT
- Elizabeth 106
- Matthias 106
- William 106

MARROW
- Carter B. 1
- John C. 14
- Mary A. T. 14
- Roxanna A. 1
- Samuel 8
- Sarah K. 104
- W. C. 14
- Willie 12
- Wm. C. 14

MARSHALL
- Johnnie Mae 79

MASON
- Flora Belle 46
- John Oley 55
- Linnie R. 64
- Martha Anne 55
- Powell W. 46
- Thomas Henry 46
- Violet Parker 46

MAST
- Elsie Lucille 125
- Emma C. 124
- John Z. 124
- Lizzie M. 124
- Rebecca Edna 124
- Sarah Leta 125

MATER
- Jake 95
- Rosa 95

MAYNARD
- Jennett Lawton 71

MAYO
- Frederick Allen ... 3

McCANN
- Lee 113

McCULLACK
- Sarah Alice 120

McINTOSH
- A. L. 58
- John M. 43
- John M. 63
- Margie 47
- Rosa Etta 58
- Sammuel Y. 48
- William S. 58

MELZER
- Anna 47
- Charles 47

MENCH
- Hudson 119
- Sally 119
- W. F. 119

MESSICK
- Frances W. 79
- M. Cecil 79
- Mary Treslyn 79
- May Dozier 79

MILLER
- Abbie M. 124
- Abi Virginia 124
- Christian K. 124
- J. R. 126
- Magdalena 126
- Nancy J. 131
- Nathaniel Fleming . 119
- Sue E. 120

MILLICOTT
- Margaret E. 64

MILLS
- Catherine I. Heywood ... 64
- Herbert 8
- Maggie 8

MILNER
- Mary 100
- Thomas 100

MILSTEAD
- Emmett Ward 79
- Nannie Wynne 79

MINER
- Ann Eliza 79
- Christopher 80
- Henry C. 79
- Mary 79, 80
- Matilda 80
- S. H. 79, 80
- S. L. 79
- Sam'l Carter 80
- Sam'l Hyde 79, 80
- Samuel H. 79
- Sarah L. 80
- W. C. 80
- William C. 79, 80
- Winslow H. 80
- Wm. Christopher ... 79

MITCHELL
- Clara Virginia 95
- Joseph T. 118
- Thomas B. 95

MOLLER
- Folmer H. 80
- Helen B. 80

MONTAGUE
- J. H. 16

MOODEY
- Peter 12

MOODY
- Adline 11

MOORE
- Alexander 5
- Charles 104, 106
- F. M. 80
- Harry S. 4
- Harry W. 4
- Isabella Farmer ... 5
- John Filmer 106
- Joseph Samuel 80
- Louise Walker 4
- Martha 106
- Ralph Haywood 80
- Samuel E. 4
- Solomon A. 4
- Thomas 113
- W. F. 80
- Warner F. 80
- William H. 4

MORGAN
- Daisy Moore 51
- J. W. 49
- John William 51
- Reginald 51
- Sarah Walters 51
- Wemmie Rowe 49

MORROW
- Emma 12

MUNSON
- Mary Letha 52

MURY
- Mary Ellen 120

NAZARETH
- Chauncy V. 6
- Iadare L. 6
- Johnnie E. 6
- Juanita Stokes 6
- Robert E. 6
- Robert H. 6
- Robert Henry 11

NAZARTH
- Bertie 11

NEIL
- Edward O. 113

NELSON
- Lugie A. 10

NETTLES
- Edward Filmore 80
- Mary Crafford 80

No Name 39

NORMAN
- Joseph 113

NORTHROP
- Carrie Jones 64
- Cora B. 64

OH
- Kwang Boon 40

OWENS
- Acie A. 59
- Bessie 61

Bettie E. 50	Thomas E. 56	Cora Lee 46
Edward T. 52	**PHILLIPS**	Emeline Elizabeth 56
Hattie B. 59	Estelle 8	Thomas F. 56
Lille O. 52	**POOLE**	William C. 46
M. C. 61	A. W. 10	**RUSSELL**
Martha 7	Anthony M. 10	Edward S. 27
William A. 50	Lucy F. 10	Thomas C. 26
PAENG	**POWELL**	**SAKAI**
Kathleen Ilkyong 40	Mary Zella 96	Takeharu 40
PALACK	**REECE**	**SATTERFIELD**
Joseph J 53	Agnes 11	James H. 83
Laura Fox 53	Moses 11	**SAUNDERS**
PALLACK 53	Nettie 11	Laura J. 94
PARKER	W. T. 11	Lillie 96
Annie Bell 46	**REED**	Maud H. 95
C. W. 44, 54	Arthur 9	Sarah A. 95
Catherine W. 3	Dorothy 2	Thomas 95
Earl Arthur 61	John Bertram 81	Thomas L. 94
Eather O. 55	Josephine W. 9	William B. 95
Edward L. 62	Kissiah 3	William Wesley 95
Edward T. 47	Laura Virginia 81	Winfred L. 94
George 5	Martha 1	**SAVAGE**
Irene P. 9	Spencer 8	Alice 82
Irma Topping 46	**REYNOLDS**	J. B. 82
John Edward 46	Oakey R. 113	**SAWYER**
John L. 55	**RICHARDSON**	Alice Skillman 82
John Revel 46	Addie L. McGuire 81	Julia Faye 82
Joseph Daniel 46	Allen Dawson 81	William Lee 82
Josephine 5	**RIGGLE**	**SCHELL**
Margaret S. 47	Abraham 81	Clara Estelle 82
Milton L. 6	Daisy M. 81	**SCHMIDT**
Mingo 3	Earl A. 81	Frederick 82
Sarah Jane Fox 46	**RIPLEY**	**SCOTT**
Thomas H. 62	Alexina S. 81	John 4
Victor F. 61	Beatrice 82	Lillie 9
PARRISH	Clyde H. 81	Oliver R. 83
Ernest L. 81	Coleman F. 81, 82	**SCRIMINGER** 58
Janie 81	Douglas C. 81	Cora H. 58
Omer 81	Ella 81	H. C. 58
PATRICK	George 82	Hettie 58
Daniel C. 38	George W. 81	J. E. 44
Daniel O. 38	Harry C. 82	J. H. 59
Elizabeth 63	James A. 82	Jane 46
Fitzhugh 63	James C. 82	Julius L. 59
Freddie 63	Mary A. 82	Sarah V. 44
Julia 38	Mattie I. 82	Sarah V. 59
Julia G. 38	Nellie B. 82	**SEAWARISHT**
PAXSON	Rebecca 81	Clareave 9
Carolyn S. 58	Virginia 81	**SEAY**
Norris H. 58	**ROBERTS**	John B. 119
PEARSON	Asia R. 5	**SEBURN**
Albert W. 3	Noble E. 82	Franklin 49
PERDY	Robert L. 82	**SENDER**
Marjorie Clarice 9	**ROBINSON**	Richard A. 40
PETERS	Clifton 10	**SHACKELFORD**
Benjamin F. 50	Deborah L. 8	Maggie 49
Benjamin F. 50	Lottie V. 2	**SHANKLAND**
Edmond F. 50	**ROLVIX**	Archie 120
Lottie H. 51	Britt 57	**SHEILD**
Mary E. 50	**ROSCOW**	John Archer 83
Matthew 50	Mary 134	Sally Cooke 83
Sarah F. 50	William 134	**SHELLEY**
W. M. 120	**ROSE**	Henry 123
William G. 51	James W. 113	Jacob H. 123
PHAUP	**ROSS**	Martha H. 123
Ernest 55	Adline 12	Mary 123
Georgie Turlington 49	H. H. 12	**SHENE**
Mary H. 56	**ROWE**	Carrie Norton 128

SHENK
    Ralph Arnold 128
SHENK
    Catharine 131
    Fannie V. 131
    Martin B. 131
SHEPHERD
    Birdie Aphia 83
    D. S. 83
SHIELDS
    Annie B. 10
SIMMONS
    William E. 113
SIMONSON
    Clinton 120
SKILLMAN
    Benjamin R. 83
    G. Gilbert 83
    Julia A. 83
    Sara Williams 83
SKINNER
    Judith 27
    Saml. 27
SMITH
    Aaron 11
    Alexander 3
    Alexina "Lady" 81
    Annie Curtis 108
    Bessie 3
    Bessie 16
    Catharine 1
    Charles Edward 119
    Elizabeth A. 51
    George Levin 108
    Henrettta 11
    Lucinda 83
    Marion T. 4
    Milan 83
    Millie 11
    Richard 11
    Samuel G. 53
    Sara 11
    Vectoria 6
    William 11
SMOKER
    Alta M. 124
    Wilbur H 124
SMUCKER
    Loran J. 126
SO
    Yong Kap 40
SPENCER
    Alexander E. 7
    Evelyn N. 7
    Henry D. 7
    Patti Vivian Pointer 7
    Robert Wyatt 7
    Sarah Jane 8
    Vivian A. 8
    Wyatt 7
SPRATLEY
    J. N. 10
    Rosanna 10
SREVES
    Albert W. 60
    Aldicut W. 53
STOKES
    James 113
    Melba C. 8

SWANN
    Anthony 8
SWANSON
    Daniel J. 83
SWEENEY
    Nancy C. 83
SWINERTON
    John Robinson 119
SYKES
    Allen James 44
    Ellen James 54
SYNDER
    John Lee 115
TABB
    Edward 43, 54
    Fannie E. 44, 57
    France W. 43
    Francis W. 53
    John E. 57
    John L. 44
    John L. 57
    Sarah Lucas 54
TALTON
    Bertha P. 5
    Claude C. 5
    Delia 7
    Elizabeth L. 4, 5
    Ellis H. 8
    Eva V. 5
    Isaac E. 5
    James 5
    Lucy A. 2
    Solomon 7
    Watt 7
    Wilbert 3
TAYLOR
    Annie E. 51
    Dora Lee 6
    Frank 51
    Jacqueline 10
    John D. 51
    John H. 51
    Josephine 3
    Samuel 3
    W. Howard 51
TENNIS
    F. L. 84
    Frederick H. 84
    Frederick Lee 84
    R. Fitchett 84
TERRELL
    Frank D. 84
THACKER
    J. T. 84
THOMAS
    Alberta 10
    Christopher 10
    Ellen 8
    Jerry 12
    Jerry 11
    John 8
    Mary 12
    Mattie 10
THOMPSON
    Jno. 66
THORNTON
    Pauline D. 2
TILLERY

TILLOT
    Ruth 7
TILLOT
    Charles F. 43
    Charles T. 59
    William H. 43
    William H. 59
TOLEY
    Frank J. 113
TOWNS
    Lewis 113
TRISSUE
    Clyde 113
TRUMAN
    Grace 62
TRUMBLE
    Isaiah 6
    John 5
    Stanley 5
TURLINGTON
    Andrew J. 50
    Annie R. 54
    B. F. 49
    Grace F. 49
    Robert L. 49
    W. H. 50
    Willie T. 51
TURNER
    E. A. 93
    E. A. 94
    Elizabeth Anne 94
    Infant 94
    Infant son 93
    Stephen 93
    Stephen 94
    William H. 94
Unknown
    Baby 52
VAIL
    Edward J. 61
VERNON
    Charles T. 120
WAGONER
    Leo S. 84
WAID
    James Willard 84
WALKER
    Burleigh Harrison 54
    Fannie 11
    James A 4
    Robert 4
    Russell Clayton 54
    Ruth Campbell 54
    Sussannah M. Newman . . 84
    William 4
    William A. 11
    William B. 11
WALLER
    Edmund 106
    Mary Ann 106
    Mary E. F. 104
WALSH
    Emma C. 84
    Leroy C. 84
WALTERS
    Gloria A. 64
    John J. 63
    John W. 63
    Martha Jane 63

WARD (cont.)
    Martha L. 63
    Nettie M. 64
    Thomas W. 64
WARDEN
    William E. 8
WASHINGTON
    Lucy 3
WATKINS
    Leola V. 1
WATSON
    Robert W. 93
    Sarah B. 27
WEITZ
    Elizabeth 120
WELL
    Horace 2
WELLS
    Ada G. 59
    Blanche 2
    Henderson 1
    Jimmie P. 1
    Laura G. 1
WEST
    Alexander D. 84
    Anna Mary 84
    Samuel K. 84
    Virginia K. 84
WEYMOUTH
    Robt. Y. 38
WHISPELL
    Maggie Parker 54
WHITAKER
    William C. 84
WHITE
    Christean W. 1
    Deacon J. M. 1
    Janna 1
    Lola P. 62
    Lucy Ray 62
    Paul A. 62
    Pelham A. 62
    Robert E. 62
    Rosa 8
WILLIAM
    Arthur 3
    Thomas C. 3
WILLIAMS
    Adelia T. 7
    Alma O. 9
    Ben H. 55
    Edna Parker 5
    Estelle 5
    Lenard T. 7
    Margaret 119
    Mary 84
WILLIAMSON
    James C. 84
    Nannie Curtis 84
WILLIS
    Charles G. 85
WILSON
    Annie Louise 93
    Bernice A. 2
    Daughter 134
    George D. 95
    Hezzie L. 2
    M. L. 96
    Maria L. 96

    Mary 100
    Mattie 93
    Richard 96
    Robt 93
    Walker W. 96
    Wilton J. 96
    Wm. 100
    Wm. 134
WOODFIN
    Floyd R. 46
    Sarah H. 46
WOODLAND
    William L. 130
WOOTEN
    Bettie 85
    J. T. 85
    John T. 85
    Mary D. 85
WRIGHT
    Carrington F. 115
    Gladys Pearl 56
    Jessie 43, 50
    Margaret L. 116
    Roberta 50
    Roberta I. 43
    Samuel D. 115
    Thomas D. 109
WYATT
    Mary S. 93
    Robert W. 93
WYNFREY
    Minnie M. 2
WYNNE
    M. A. 2
    Baker P. 85
    Barney E. 6
    Bettie H. 85
    Effie Cary 85
    Eliza 3
    Hannah Mahala 85
    L. L. 2
    Miles 3
    Miles Wills 85
    Nina V. 85
    Richard C. 104, 105
    Robert Baker 85
    Rogert T. 86
    Sarah 105
    Sarah A. 106
    Tho. G. 85
    Wm. B. 85
YEAGER
    Avis Dale 85
    Junior Clay 85
YODER
    Clarence P. 126
    David S. 123
    Elizabeth B. 126
    Ella M. 123
    Izetta B. 126
    Johny D. 123
    Malinda 123
    Melvin J. 123
    Simon P. 131
YOUNG
    Ann Green 136
    Ann Warwick 136
    Anne B. {Benson} 136

    Elizabeth McMcoy 136
    George B. 136
    John Alden 55
    John H. 89
    William G. 136
    William G. {Garrow} .. 135
ZOOK
    Joel 124
    Joseph 124
    Sallie 124
ZVERCHER
    Edna I. 125
    Elliott H. 125